PERMANENT
VACATIO

# CODY SIMPSON

WELCOME TO PARADISE:
MY JOURNEY

# CODY SIMPSON

WELCOME TO PARADISE:
MY JOURNEY

## 100% OFFICIAL

I WANT TO DEDICATE THIS BOOK
TO MY FAMILY FOR MAKING ME
THE YOUNG MAN I AM TODAY AND
FOR ALLOWING ME TO PURSUE
MY DREAMS. I ALSO WANT TO
DEDICATE THIS BOOK TO ALL OF
MY ANGELS FOR BELIEVING IN
ME AND HELPING ME MAKE MY
DREAMS BECOME A REALITY.

Dedication

Introd

# WELCOME TO PARADISE

I stand behind the heavy curtain, waiting. The energy of the crowd is palpable in the air. The O2 Arena in London is swelling with nearly 20,000 fans. This is going to be the biggest concert of my life! And I can't wait to get out on stage and give them all I have. I wait to take the stage, and think about how far I am from my beach-town roots in Australia. I am halfway around the world and about to perform in front of a huge crowd. I roll up onto the balls of my feet, adrenalin just surging through every cell in my body. It's nearly time!

I hear the music starting, my cue. It's my last moment of calm before the storm. I turn to my security guard Jeff and we do our handshake, like always, before I go out on stage. I take a few steps and feel the heat of the bright lights and the power of the audience's screams.

'It's such an honour to be here this evening! I want to thank my mate Justin Bieber for having me here in London. And I want to thank all these beautiful fans for coming out tonight. Before I get started, I'd like to introduce myself. My name is Cody Simpson.'

BEFORE I GET STARTED, I'D LIKE TO INTRODUCE MYSELF. MY NAME IS CODY SIMPSON

I'VE ALREADY COME A LONG WAY – FROM THE BEACHES OF AUSTRALIA TO THE BRIGHT LIGHTS OF HOLLYWOOD – AND I HAVE A SHOT TO LEAVE MY MARK ON THE MUSIC WORLD

I have always dreamed big, but I never grew up dreaming of being a pop star. Instead, my sights were set on achieving the highest honours in competitive swimming – Olympic gold medals.

My love of the water began when I was just a few years old when my parents started taking me to swimming pools and the beach. I started swimming competitively at the age of nine and I had a natural ability, even though I was smaller and scrawnier than the other kids. I was clearly the underdog, but I worked the hardest at our practices and when I went to my first competition with my local swimming club, Miami Swim Club, I won every race. That feeling of winning after training so hard was imprinted on me from that day on. I knew anything was possible if you worked hard enough for it.

That underdog mentality has fuelled me. I never lost that drive. And eventually I even made it to the Australian Schools Swimming Nationals and won most of my events. I like to push myself to achieve new goals. I set high standards for myself. Working hard just feels natural to me. I don't know how to not be the way I am. Ever since I was a youngster, I've wanted to be something extraordinary. I was never content with coming second in a race, or not trying my best. I'm still not. I always push myself to the limit.

Music came to me just as naturally as swimming. My parents introduced me to music early on. Around the house or at family gatherings, my family and friends regularly pulled out guitars and sang along to the classic country songs by Hank Williams and Johnny Cash. I loved to sit with them and feel a part of the music, even before I knew how to play guitar.

Now I'm on this incredible journey. I've already come a long way – from the beaches of Australia to the bright lights of Hollywood – and I have a shot to leave my mark on the music world. This book is a look back at my journey here, from the beginning. Like any meaningful achievement, getting to this point came with a lot of sacrifices and a lot of tough

# MY MUSIC IS FOR EVERYONE WHO HAS TAKEN THIS JOURNEY WITH ME

choices. I also know that I have worked long and hard to get here. And that might be the best feeling there is: to put in the work and see it pay off when you start achieving your goals.

People always ask: would you rather have a gold medal or a platinum record? My answer is the platinum record. Both require tremendous work and great risk – but, honestly, you can't share a gold medal. My music is for everyone who has taken this journey with me.

You, the fans, have been there for me every step of the way, and now it's my turn to give something back to you. I want my fans to understand me and my story. As an artist, it's hard to show people all of the different parts that make you who you really are. This is my chance to lift the curtain and invite all of you inside my world, to see my journey and the choices that led me here – to paradise.

# Gold Coast

## CHAPTER ONE

### Coast

#### innings

# THE MAKING OF ME

Where we come from can have a huge impact on who we are. It sure did for me. I was born on 11 January 1997, in paradise. Actually, where I was born just feels like paradise: the Gold Coast, an ocean-side city on the south-east edge of Queensland, Australia. I grew up in a surfing culture and that laid-back mentality runs deep in my blood. Even though I've lived in Los Angeles for over three years, I still see my Gold Coast attitude coming through in nearly everything I do.

My hometown is closer to Tokyo and Bangkok than it is to Los Angeles, New York, or London. The area exploded in the 1980s as a hot destination for surfers, and just before I was born it became the second most populated area in Queensland, after Brisbane. It remains a major tourist spot; we've got a great subtropical climate, theme parks, nightlife, and a rainforest nearby – so naturally people love it. It's rarely below 50 degrees, even in winter.

While I was growing up, Dad worked as a stockbroker and later owned his own investment company. Mum stayed home to look after us kids. After me, there's my sister Alli, born just 15 months later. Mum certainly had her hands full with us! She says it was kind of like raising twins, because we were

MUM CERTAINLY HAD HER HANDS FULL WITH US! SHE SAYS IT WAS KIND OF LIKE RAISING TWINS, BECAUSE WE WERE SO CLOSE TOGETHER IN AGE

Clockwise from top left: With Mum and Alli in the Whitsunday Islands, Australia; 'selfies' with Tom; my first date! with Madi Marr; baking day with Alli.

so close together in age. We tended to share everything and even had the same friends as we grew up. I would also look out for Alli, always making sure she was okay. She is my little sister, after all.

And then Tom came along seven years after me. I remember how excited Alli and I were the day he was born. We went straight to the hospital after school to see him. It was pretty cool for Alli and me to have another sibling, another Simpson.

Mum is amazing, so nurturing, and always there, caring for us. We had a nice, comfortable house in a cool beachside community called Mermaid Waters where, when I was old enough, I could grab my mates and hit the surf whenever I wanted.

My life was always very family-oriented and I really like that. Mum's side of the family lived nearby on the Gold

Coast, and Dad's family lived just an hour or so north, in Brisbane. We're extremely close – as close as a family can be.

I saw my grandparents and cousins almost every weekend, and we had regular family dinners. We celebrated holidays and birthdays all together, taking turns at different houses. Both of my grandmas, all of my aunts, and my mum would make dishes and bring them over for holidays, so we'd always have a big feast.

I'm especially close to my mum's parents, who I call Nanna and Poppa, as they lived very nearby and I'd stay over at their house regularly. Poppa and I share the same birthday, so we've always celebrated together. Nanna makes my absolute favourite dessert, called pavlova. It's meringue underneath, with sweet foam, cream and fruit on top. It's like heaven! She always makes it on my birthday and on holidays. That dessert and Grandma's homemade chocolate delights are things I really look forward to when I go home for a visit.

Clockwise from top left: Family holiday in the Whitsundays; groovy grandmothers; visiting cousin Kai at school; in the Bahamas meeting the extended family!

We're in opposite seasons to the States and Europe, which means that Christmas is actually during the summertime in Australia, and at the end of December it's very hot. So around the holiday we'd spend a lot of time outside, surfing and skateboarding, trying out new gifts, instead of nestled by the fire with cocoa. Summer is always so hot that most of what we would do was focused on water and staying cool. Christmas Day was usually spent in our bathing suits – we call them togs – all day long. We would be in the pool or at the beach, then dry off and eat, then get back in immediately. And we tend to serve cold dishes, because it is just too hot for anything else. So we'd have seafood, such as grilled shrimp, and salads and cold ham rather than the traditional turkey with all the trimmings. Another of my favourite dishes at Christmas is Great Nanna's famous Western Samoan Chop Suey recipe. Poppa was born in Samoa and we have this dish at all our family gatherings to keep the tradition alive.

One Christmas, when I was seven years old, I got a brand-new BMX bike. There's a BMX track outside my house, so that morning my cousins and I ran straight outside to try it out on the track. I wiped out pretty hard and nearly broke my wrist, so instead of eating our holiday meal at home we spent the afternoon in the hospital getting it checked out.

For my family, it was all about being outside and being adventurous. From BMXing to surfing – we spent a lot of time together in the outdoors. It's just the Gold Coast culture. Everyone lives and breathes the ocean and surfing. I learned to surf at nine years old. My dad, Uncle John, and even Poppa all surf.

We moved a few times within the Gold Coast, because my parents used to buy apartments and houses, fix them up and sell them. But no matter where we lived, my bedroom always reflected my passions – a surfboard in one corner, a guitar in the other corner, with a big Australian flag on one

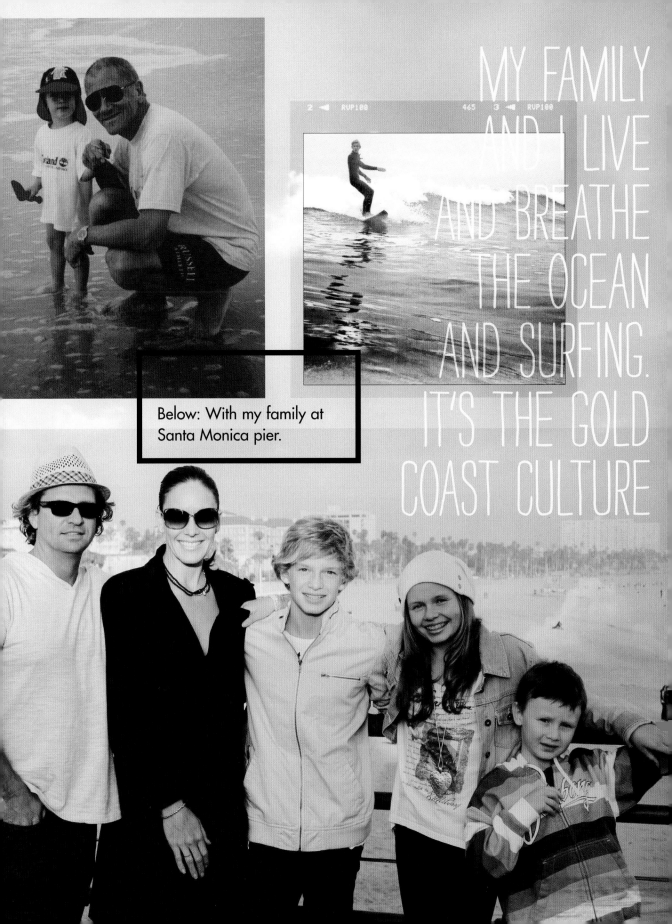

MY FAMILY AND I LIVE AND BREATHE THE OCEAN AND SURFING. IT'S THE GOLD COAST CULTURE

Below: With my family at Santa Monica pier.

I FEEL SO BLESSED
THAT MY PARENTS,
GRANDPARENTS
AND ENTIRE
FAMILY CREATED
AN ENVIRONMENT
WHERE WE KIDS
COULD ALL THINK BIG

Above: Early surfing days on the Gold Coast. Right: Big family gatherings.

of the walls and surf posters on the others. I love to be surrounded by the things that make me happy.

My family were always very encouraging. When I was eight or nine, Nanna asked me what I was going to do when I grew up. I answered: 'I'm going to be really famous and successful, but I just don't know at what yet.' Nanna said she got goose bumps when I said it. My family encouraged my big dreams even when I wasn't sure what my goals were, but especially when I homed in on what I was passionate about. I feel so blessed that my parents, grandparents, and entire extended family created an environment where we kids could all think big.

My whole family follows my music career pretty closely. They've always supported me, and our decision to leave Australia. They are always telling me how proud they are of me. It means a lot to me to know that I have them behind me.

Alli and I have always had loads in common. We spent a lot of time together when we were growing up. We're probably closer than the average brother and sister. We've had our arguments and, like many brothers and sisters, we've fought over trivial things, especially when we were young. But we never let it go too far. We wind up feeling bad for each other and it always ends up as a joke. And now, since we moved away from home, we hardly ever argue and generally rely on each other pretty much as best friends.

Alli used to get annoyed because I used to sing nonstop. I'd have a song in my head and just sing it around the house, over and over again. She'd be doing her maths homework or concentrating on something at the kitchen table and I'd walk by singing, and she'd yell for me to stop. Actually, she still gets annoyed at me for doing this!

Our parents were always pretty protective of us. They still are – especially here in the States – and I wouldn't have it any other way. I really respect my parents and their decisions, and I don't hassle them about saying no to something. My

Clockwise from top: Dad and I at the Jingle Ball; Alli and I on the tour bus; dressed to impress at the G'Day LA gala ball; 'selfies' with good mates.

ALLI AND I HAVE ALWAYS HAD LOADS IN COMMON. WE SPENT A LOT OF TIME TOGETHER WHEN WE WERE GROWING UP

dad tends to be more laid-back than my mum. My mum is a little quieter around new people and in new situations, while my dad is more open and talkative right off the bat. I'm naturally a little quieter, like my mum, but once I feel comfortable, then I'm more outgoing and open like my dad.

As a kid, I was pretty shy; it took a while for me to trust people and come out of my shell. So I'd always be sort of hiding behind my mum when I was around new people. But once I warmed up, I'd be running around. Alli would probably say that I'm not really silly around anyone until I have spent a decent amount of time with them first.

But that innate shyness never got in the way of my love of being onstage. As kids, Alli and I would always do little performances together at family gatherings, where we'd make up

# THAT INNATE SHYNESS NEVER GOT IN THE WAY OF MY LOVE OF BEING ONSTAGE

a dance or I would sing and Alli would dance. We used to go into full costume for these, and my parents and whatever family members were around would sit patiently and watch our little show, clapping and going on like we were the greatest. We liked to film ourselves and watch it over and over again. We loved it! We'd even do our musical performances on my grandparents' boat, when they took the family out.

Our very good family friends from the Gold Coast, the Baildons, were always around for these shows. Andrew and Karen Baildon are the best friends of my parents, and their kids Yasmin and Flynn are close with me and Alli. We all grew up together and spent most weekends together. Alli, Yasmin, Flynn, and I would put on concerts and perform dances and skits.

I was all laughs when we goofed around at home, but I took school much more seriously, even during grade school and junior high. I gravitated more towards English and creative subjects, but I still tried my best in maths and science. I was generally well behaved in school and somewhat quiet. And I was a perfectionist from an early age. When it came to my schoolwork, when it got to looking too messy or when my handwriting wasn't up to par, I would erase the whole thing and redo it. My teachers used to get mad at me for that! I guess I was over-thinking things a bit. I just always remember wanting things to be done perfectly.

# SWIMMING DREAMS

I started taking swimming lessons when I was six years old at the Baildons' Superfish Swim School. I was immediately very comfortable in the water. I took to it right away. Andrew Baildon, who was an Olympic swimmer himself, saw some potential in me and was a great mentor for me from an early age.

It was only natural for me to want to take it to the next level, and when I was eight years old I signed up under elite coach Denis Cotterell at the Miami Swim Club. Denis had coached my mum and Andrew and many other Olympians and world record holders, so it meant a lot to me to be able to train under him.

When I was young, the swimming team was a lot of fun and a good way to set goals and work towards something. I think my love of goals and hard work comes from my parents. They always told me it was important to work hard and try your best. And they knew what they were talking about. My mum and dad swam competitively themselves, and they both made it pretty far in the national competitive circuit. It's remarkable to me that my mum and dad competed at such an elite level! My mum swam in the Pan Pacific Games and was ranked seventh in the world, and my dad was an

Australian champion. They both were number one overall for certain events in Australia – Mum in the 100 and 200 metres breaststroke, and Dad in the 200 metres breaststroke – but they both got injured and didn't make it to the Olympics to represent Australia.

They don't dwell on what might have been, but I think there was an extra gleam in their eye when I started to pursue the sport. They were clearly thrilled that I was passionate about swimming and reached a competitive level. Their sense of discipline must have sunk in at some point, because even at just nine years old I really put my heart into improving at swimming.

I practised three to four times a week. My races would be just 25 metres, but at the time it all felt very important – and, of course, fun. Two years later, I swam in my first race and won it. It was a big moment for me. I was so proud of myself, and my parents ran over to me after the race to celebrate! I felt the energy of the cheers during the race and the excitement of winning for days afterwards. I still have the ribbon from that first race. From then on, I was hooked!

We had swimming meets every other weekend in the summer, and almost as frequently in the winter as well. As I became more competitive, it became a year-round sport for me. I loved the thrill of racing from an early age. At the meets I also loved messing about with my friends and eating the good food they had at the pool café. My closest friends were always people I met through swimming. I still keep in touch with quite a few of them and they often come over to Los Angeles to stay and hang out with me.

I was a late bloomer and I felt fairly small standing beside some of the kids who had early growth spurts. I think it just made me that much more determined. I've always been very competitive, but I'm never a sore loser. I'm always gracious in defeat. I think how a person is when they lose shows a lot about their character.

Above: Going for gold at the Gold Coast Swimming Championships. Right: Feeling like an Olympian with Grant Hackett's Olympic medals.

MY LOVE OF GOALS AND HARD WORK COMES FROM MY PARENTS

# MUSICAL BEGINNINGS

Just as the surf and swimming culture was a passion of mine from the very beginning, music has been a part of my life for as long as I can remember. Whenever we would get together with family and friends, it seems like we always ended up around a bonfire or a dinner table playing and singing along to our favourite songs. We hosted these barbecues and parties with close family friends, and they would bring their guitars and we'd all gather round and sing songs. Everyone would join in and I remember sitting next to my parents, in this big circle, and loving the sound of all of our voices mixing together.

We mostly played country music, classics by Johnny Cash and Hank Williams, and sometimes a little Elvis was thrown into the mix. When I was six, I really fell in love with country music. I loved the sound of the tinny guitars and how the songs were more like stories. There was really a journey unfolding in each one, full of emotion and layers. It set a high bar for me when I began to write my own songs.

Clockwise from top: Entertaining with Dad, age eight; my first pretend guitar; my early efforts at finger picking.

MUSIC HAS BEEN PART OF MY LIFE
FOR AS LONG AS I CAN REMEMBER

My first concert memory is from when I was nine or ten years old and we went to the Brisbane Entertainment Centre to see Keith Urban. The whole family went, along with all four of my grandparents, and I brought a friend of mine, too. We had great seats, close to the stage, and I was jumping and screaming and singing along. I was in awe. I realised then the power of connecting to an audience through music. Playing together had always connected my family and close friends, but now I saw Keith Urban connect to thousands and thousands of fans at once. It was powerful.

Country music was pretty much all we listened to around the house and played as a family when I was young. My grandparents had passed their love of country music on to my dad, and at home he always had his guitar in hand and was always strumming away at some chords or breaking into a song. No wonder I'm always walking around singing!

Of course, I wanted to learn how to play guitar so I could join him. I asked for a guitar for my sixth birthday and my grandparents gave me a quarter-size one. I was thrilled! I signed up for lessons immediately. 'Jackson' by Johnny Cash was one of the first songs I learned to play on the guitar. It only had three chords, and those were the only chords I knew. But I played that song all the time. I couldn't wait to join in on those impromptu jam sessions around the barbecue. And – just like my dad – the guitar rarely left my hands.

# MUSIC HAS THE POWER TO CONNECT PEOPLE

# Two Loves

## CHAPTER TWO

# PITCH PERFECT

Swimming and music were my whole world. If I wasn't in the pool training, I was sitting on my bed practising the guitar and writing songs. Swimming was serious for me, whereas music was more fun, with less pressure. I enjoyed swimming because it was competitive, while music was more of a passion. I was doing it because I liked it.

My parents signed me up for private guitar lessons at a nearby guitar shop. During one of my first lessons, the teacher had me turn around while he played and asked me if I could pick out the notes by ear. He would play a single note – a G, say, or a B or a C – and I was able to pick it out accurately. He was pretty shocked. After the lesson, he took my parents aside for a private chat, and he told them that it was quite rare for someone my age to be able to identify notes like that. That's when they first realised that I had a natural feel for the guitar and an ear for music. Meanwhile, I was sitting outside the lesson room thinking, 'What did I do wrong?!'

I started taking lessons on and off over the next few years, sometimes stopping for a while because of swimming commitments. When I wasn't in lessons, I was still playing non-stop. Even if I didn't know the chords or what I was

doing, I just kept at it. My dad would take out his guitar and we'd sit together plucking out notes to a song until I could play along with him. Alli sings a bit but doesn't play any instruments, and Tom appears to be interested in music now, but he's still young, so we'll see what he gets into. Right now, he is just having fun travelling and being a kid.

When I took lessons, I went weekly, but I still didn't practise regularly. It was more of a fun hobby and my focus was on swimming. I would teach myself a lot by ear, and I went online to look up chords and fingerings and figured it out from there. My lessons started out focused a lot on music theory, genres, and composers, and notation, but I didn't always like it. I wanted to play my favourite songs by Keith Urban and Johnny Cash, and I didn't always care about the theories and correct techniques. So my parents spoke to the guitar teacher, and he agreed to let me bring in my favourite songs and structure the lessons around them. This way of learning kept me interested in playing and made it much more fun.

I wrote my first song when I was eight years old, and it was called 'Further Away From Me'. Well, actually, I wrote my first song when I was six, and it was about putting diapers on a chicken, but I would prefer not to be remembered for that one. 'Further Away From Me' was a bit better than that. It was about the feeling of drifting away from a girl, and not being able to keep the relationship going. It was a mature song for my age! I played it for my parents when it was finished and they thought it was good, but a little too mature. They wondered about where I was getting my inspiration. But the truth is, I have been into girls for as long as I can remember!

When I start doing something and see that I'm good at it, I want to keep going. I started writing more songs and playing them for my family, who encouraged me. That's when I started to develop the confidence to play in front of different people, including our family and friends when we all got together.

Left: Recording my single 'Pretty Brown Eyes'. Below: Launching into Justin Bieber's Believe tour.

The process of writing a song developed naturally as I was learning the guitar. I spent a lot of time teaching myself when I was in between lessons. Making up melodies and adding words felt like a natural next step. I would start with some chords that I learned in lessons, and from there I would go online and look up how to play other chords and notes. Once I had the chords I thought I needed, I would just start singing tunes to it. Writing the lyrics was always the last thing I did. I still use pretty much the same process. I really enjoy just playing guitar and humming a great melody. Now, once I have that down, I record it on my phone, and then start working on the lyrics.

Songwriting has become an important way for me to express myself. As I've got older, and experienced some exciting and confusing situations with girls, I've found it a powerful outlet for me to work through my feelings. When I think I have a good story, I'll write a song to it. And sometimes the opposite happens – I'm just playing on the guitar, and I'm coming up with a cool chord progression, and then the song develops from there.

My songs can be very personal and, being a bit shy, I only played my original songs for my family and grandparents. I didn't even play them for friends. My family encouraged me 100 per cent and as time went on I started getting the confidence to play in front of different people. Eventually I worked up the courage to play some of my own songs when we were all gathered outside at one of our barbecues.

It felt good to be a part of that creative, musical circle of adults. A good family friend, Brett Penwarn, is a terrific guitarist and singer. He was also our family doctor. Alli and I are close to his kids, too – Jasmin and Brayden. He always came over for jam sessions, and I looked up to him quite a bit. I always thought he was an amazing musician and, when I was really young, I would sit next to him with my little guitar and watch him play. I stared at his fingers and tried to learn from him. I would call Brett one of my mentors in life.

SONGWRITING HAS BECOME AN IMPORTANT WAY FOR ME TO EXPRESS MYSELF

# MY SONGS CAN BE VERY PERSONAL

Soon after I started lessons, I was able to come in and pick up some of the same songs and riffs that Brett was playing. It felt amazing to really be a part of those moments! Of course, everyone around me was so impressed that I could pick it up so fast, so naturally that felt pretty great. And now, when I go home for a visit, we still have those jam sessions and sometimes I take the lead. Of all my musical experiences, playing really well around the barbecue can still be among the most fulfilling.

By the age of eight, I had outgrown my first guitar and needed a bigger and more professional one. I went to this guitar shop in town with my dad, and we were just browsing. I picked up a guitar I liked and started strumming on it to get a feel. Dad encouraged me to really play it and sing something with it. I had the Johnny Cash song 'Folsom Prison Blues' in my head, so I started playing and singing. The employees and guitar teachers from the store – and some other shoppers – stopped and started to listen, eventually gathering closer. I just kept playing as they grouped around me, and when I finished, everyone applauded.

That was really my first performance in front of an audience that wasn't my family. And it felt pretty great! One of the guitar teachers there specialised in country music, and he approached me afterwards and asked if I wanted to have lessons with him. So I did.

His name was Cash Backman, and he used to be a country artist in Australia. He'd even had a number one song. I worked with him for a while and it was really cool to learn from someone who had reached that level. He was teaching me a lot of country songs, which my dad liked a lot.

During that time I also began to listen to more mainstream pop music, like Justin Timberlake and Chris Brown. I always wanted to learn how to play songs by these guys on the guitar, but I was cautious about telling Cash that I wanted to change my style musically – for good reason, as it turned out, because when I eventually did, he wasn't that supportive.

One Sunday he took me along to one of his performances at a hotel about an hour and a half away in Lowood. He was going to invite me onstage with him, and I prepared four country songs to play that night: Johnny Cash's 'Folsom Prison Blues' and 'Jackson', John Denver's 'Leaving on a Jet Plane', and Hank Williams's 'Hey Good Lookin''. I was nervous in the days leading up to the concert, but I channelled that energy into practising, again and again.

My parents drove us out to the concert, and my whole family was excited for me. I was quiet in the car, just getting myself psyched and ready. It was pretty crazy that I was out there doing that! There were about a hundred people in the audience, and I couldn't wait to get started so I could put an end to the feeling of anticipation. But my nerves all melted away once I walked up onstage. As soon as I got up there and felt the energy from the crowd, I just relaxed and played my heart out. The crowd seemed to go for it, and it was a lot of fun! It didn't change my desire to learn other kinds of music, though, and I kept pushing the boundaries. Cash still only wanted me doing country. So, eventually, we went our separate ways.

Soundcheck and rehearsals on the Paradise tour.

# MY NERVES ALL MELTED AWAY ONCE I WALKED UP ONSTAGE

My next teacher, Ram Sefer, is a really well-known instructor who specialises more in rock and pop music. He was much more open to ideas. Right away he asked me to bring in a song that I wanted to learn. I used to choose one from some of my new favourite artists like Jason Mraz, Jack Johnson, and Justin Timberlake, and he would help me work through it. Then I would bring in some songs I was writing and we would collaborate on those. He definitely helped spark my interest in writing songs and he gave me a lot of confidence. It really encouraged my music to the next level. I will always be grateful to Ram for his support.

# COMPETING AT THE NATIONALS

At nine years old, after I'd been training and competing with my local swimming team, my mum thought her old coach Denis Cotterell might be able to help me get to that next level. He's one of the leading coaches in Australia, having coached many former Olympians. It was really an honour to get to meet him. I was invited to swim at his prestigious club, the Miami Swim Club. It's an amazing facility, with two Olympic-size outdoor pools and a team of respected coaches. Swimming is a big sport in Australia, naturally, since it's part of the culture, and one that we tend to do well in at the Olympics.

Denis saw the potential in me. I worked with other coaches there, but he took me under his wing, coaching me and looking out for me over the years. He'd pull me to the side during practice to give me extra pointers. It's crazy to think about how far I could have gone with swimming. Denis really believed in me and thought I could qualify for the 2016 Olympics if I found the time to train.

I loved swimming as an outlet for my competitive nature. Even in training, I was always pushing myself to outwork the kids around me, especially the kids that were older and bigger than me. I was still smaller and skinnier than the other swimmers I was competing against. I knew I would have to work that much harder than a bigger guy to achieve my goals. And so I did. I still carry that underdog mentality with me today.

I competed in my first Australian School Nationals when I was ten years old. It was held in Adelaide, the capital of South Australia, on the southern coast. I flew out there with my team, and we had a great time goofing off and sharing in the excitement on our way to the meet. This was the next level for me. It was a five-day event, where I swam several different races each day. It was a big deal for me, and of course I was nervous, but I usually try to turn nerves into adrenalin, to fuel me to stay sharp in an event and swim my hardest.

The Nationals competition is held annually for all schools in Australia, across all sports. It's the culmination of a whole year of racing and events. Before being able to compete in them, I first had to place in my events at the local meets, and then at the State competition to make the cut. From my results at the State competition, I was ranked first or second in a lot of events.

My whole family came with me to the Nationals competition, which helped me feel comfortable. A couple of friends from my local club also made the Nationals squad, so it was great to go with them. I was the youngest on the team. As always, I felt like I had a lot to prove to keep up with my teammates. But I wouldn't have it any other way.

Before a race, we would be lined up in a holding room, waiting for our turn to walk out to the pool deck and take our positions. I would bring music and lose myself in some of my favourite songs. To race, we would all wear the Fastskin suits, which are knee-length swimming trunks that glide through the water better than normal swimming togs. While waiting, we would have on the big, warm team coats that look a bit like what boxers wear. And sometimes we would wear Ugg boots to stay warmed up for the race.

Right: A champion!
Below: Checking the results at the end of my race at the Queensland Championships.

I KNEW I WOULD HAVE TO WORK MUCH HARDER THAN A BIGGER GUY TO ACHIEVE MY GOALS

# I WAS IMMEDIATELY VERY COMFORTABLE IN THE WATER. I TOOK TO IT RIGHT AWAY

When we'd finally move from the holding room out onto the pool deck and get down to our suits, the adrenalin would really hit me. I'd climb onto the starting block and adjust my suit, then my goggles. I'd go over the race in my head, visualising every stroke and turn. I can still hear the judge telling us to take our marks and feel my muscles tighten as I bend over and grab the block. The whistle would sound, and I'd hit the water. And the rest would just happen. I knew what I was doing, and what I needed to do to win.

I'd push myself to the limit as I'd race towards the final metres. And when I'd slam into the touch pad at the end, I'd immediately look up to see my time and my place. One of the best feelings in the world is looking up to see that I've won. At the Nationals competition, I had the fastest time in the 50-metre butterfly and 50-metre freestyle for a ten-year-old. I won all the races – gold medals in all of my events, in every stroke!

The Australian Nationals have a medal ceremony like the Olympics. It was a truly amazing feeling when they called my name and I stepped up onto the podium, onto the middle, tallest level. It's so gratifying to work really, really hard at something and have it pay off or to be recognised for your efforts.

On the flip side, when I came second, I would feel so disappointed. To be honest, I was never totally happy unless I

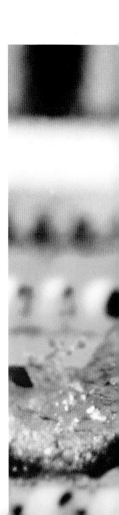

won! I know that sounds harsh, but it's a standard I set for myself. I don't like to stand on the second tier – especially when I know I could have done better. I don't like to leave anything out there.

I competed in the same competition the following year, in which I ended up with the same incredible results. When I was 12, I went to the Pan Pacific School Games, which is an even more intense and prestigious competition because it's not just Australia. More than 30 countries compete, including New Zealand, Canada, Guam and others. There I won three gold medals, two silvers and a bronze.

Swimming had all of my focus and energy. I was working really hard to reach my goals, pushing myself each and every day. I loved it. When I really thought about my future and what I wanted for myself, I hoped I could reach the Olympics. I knew that anything is possible if you work hard enough for it, and I felt like I was so close to living my dream.

Racing my favourite stroke, butterfly.

# The Making of a YouTube Star

## CHAPTER THREE

# SECRET STAR

Even while I was swimming competitively, music remained very much a fun hobby and creative outlet for me. So, when I posted my first video on YouTube, it happened by chance. I was 11 years old and there was a talent show portion of an end-of-year assembly at my school. A family friend and great friend of my sister named Nusi McCarthy had entered the talent show to sing Jason Mraz's song 'I'm Yours' a cappella. I wasn't planning to perform that night, but I offered to play guitar with her and we made it into a duet. It was fun to play for my friends at school for the first time. But it was nerve-wracking, too. I was grateful that I wasn't alone and had Nusi up there with me. The whole thing was very casual and small, though, so that made me feel more comfortable about performing. Her mum filmed the performance, and when I saw the video, I thought it was pretty cool. So I made a YouTube account and posted it online. It got a couple of hundred views and I was thrilled!

I asked my parents if I could post more videos on YouTube, and they were reluctant at first because of safety concerns. I was never allowed to have a MySpace page or even an email account. But after a few months of me bugging her, my mum started to come around. She let me sign up for MySpace and continue using my YouTube account as long as she was in control of them and could check any messages. Once she was satisfied that it was secure and safe for me to use, she even started to help me with filming and would get excited when people liked the videos.

My second video was 'Dream Catch Me' by Newton Faulkner. He's a cool surfer dude with dreadlocks, and has a great laid-back sound. It was the kind of song we would all play at our family hangouts, and in the video I sang the laid-back, beachy tune while playing along on the guitar. Mum filmed me playing and together we uploaded it to YouTube. When I watch that video now, I can't help thinking how young I look and sound!

After that, I filmed a cover of Bon Jovi's 'Wanted Dead or Alive'. In this video, you can see I'm playing it up for the camera and performing more than in the first ones. But I still hadn't had a vocal lesson at that point, and wasn't taking it too seriously.

I started to get a bit of a following – a few hundred views – and people began to ask me to put up more songs. Then my perfectionism kicked in – I had to make sure they were the best before I put them up online. I got the new guitar and I immediately recorded a new YouTube video with it: Justin Timberlake's 'Cry Me a River'. I took a singing lesson, and a month later I posted 'I Want You Back' by the Jackson 5. This video was all about the vocals; I was standing at a microphone and didn't play the guitar on it. Soon, I was getting hundreds and sometimes thousands of views. It was pretty incredible that so many people were watching my videos. I felt really flattered! Recording these videos and putting them on YouTube was something that I was doing for fun. Seeing people comment and ask for more was something I never expected!

Left: Soundchecking at Big Jingle.
Centre: Backstage at Wango Tango
at the Staples Center.

RECORDING VIDEOS
AND PUTTING
THEM ON YOUTUBE
WAS SOMETHING
I WAS DOING
FOR FUN. SEEING
PEOPLE COMMENT
AND ASK FOR MORE
WAS SOMETHING
I NEVER EXPECTED!

# I'M NOT ONE TO SHOW OFF OR BRAG TO FRIENDS

With Alli and my cousins Rae and Charlie.

At the time, I didn't take it too seriously. I didn't share much of this with my friends. I was pretty well liked in school for being an athlete – and few people even knew that I was a musician. I never liked the cliques at school. They never made sense to me, and I just sort of ignored those games. Even the music industry isn't as cliquey as school!

I worked hard on my schoolwork and I did well. Even so, the day felt very structured to me. I enjoy more creative activities, and my favourite subject was English. My parents always reminded me how important doing well in school was, so I never slacked off. My mum would drive me to school in the mornings, and sometimes I'd sing a little song that went, 'I don't want to go to school every day.'

My hard work at school paid off and I won some academic achievement awards in elementary and middle school. The last year of junior high school, I won the junior high school 'cup', which is only given to one student in the whole grade. It's for overall achievement in academics, citizenship, sports and music. It was pretty rad to win that.

That night, for the finale of the junior high award ceremony, I played the guitar and sang 'Wish You Well' by Bernard Fanning, a well-known Australian musician. It's a great, guitar-driven song. My mates came up to me afterwards and said it was awesome. That was one of the few times I played publicly in school. No one even knew about my writing or the videos. I just felt it was better to keep it all quiet. I'm not one to show off or brag to friends. So when I did this performance it felt pretty cool to share this part of me with my friends.

Around that time, my musical tastes continued to evolve and expand. I started to develop an appreciation of hip-hop, R&B and rap, including Chris Brown and Jay-Z. I didn't tell my family about my newfound enthusiasm. I just listened in my room or on headphones.

But it became apparent at my eleventh birthday party. I usually didn't have parties, but that year I had some friends over, from school and from swimming. We had this pool room in the house, and we blacked out the windows and got some strobe lights – corny, I know, but we were 11. I began playing some of my favourite songs by Michael Jackson and Justin Timberlake and, much to the surprise of my family, I started dancing. My mum saw it and noticed that I had what most people call rhythm. She – and I, for that matter – had no idea I could dance.

There was always music around when I was growing up. We were always goofing off and dancing through the house. We would have big family dance-offs or team dances to a song. It's fun to see my parents and grandparents acting silly and all doing it together.

One time, we found ourselves in the upstairs bathroom dancing to 'Marry You' by Bruno Mars. It was the whole bunch of us: my parents, me and Alli, plus both sets of my grandparents. We were dancing in the mirror and watching ourselves. Alli and I would do a dance move and then my parents and grandparents would have to copy us. We were just looking in the mirror and laughing at ourselves. It was so funny. Alli was even videoing this, so the evidence exists somewhere. I'm scared to think about watching it now!

That night sparked a few more dance parties. Our best friends would come around, and I would even find the guts to start dancing – as long as we turned all the lights off and I could sort of hide in the shadows a bit. That was only at first, though. Slowly, over the next few months, I gained a little more confidence. Everyone thought I was really good, but it took a while for me to warm up to that idea.

# MY MUSICAL TASTES CONTINUE TO EVOLVE

I loved recording videos and posting covers of some of my favourite songs. And I looked forward to seeing if I could build up more and more views with each one. Reaching a thousand views seemed like a challenge! I loved the feeling of turning on the camera and performing for an audience, even a virtual one. But that was just for fun, like our dance parties. I was totally into swimming and becoming the best I could. And to get there, I had a pretty hectic schedule for a 12-year-old.

I was training six or seven times a week in total. On some days I'd train twice a day – once in the morning and once in the evening – and on others I'd just do one session, depending on my school work. I'd get up at 4.30 a.m., and training would be from 5.30 to 7 a.m., then I'd get ready and go to school. Straight after school, I'd head to the pool to practise from 4 to 6.30 p.m., and then home to do school work. Practices were gruelling: we'd start with a 30-minute gym workout and then get in the pool.

Most of my closest friends were in my swimming club, so I liked spending time at practice. I only had a few good friends at school, but swimming mates understood the love of the sport. So it was fun, but hard – and that's just the way I like it.

# Tollywood

## CHAPTER FOUR

# Calling

# THE MESSAGE OF A LIFETIME

In May 2009, a music producer from America named Shawn Campbell found a couple of my videos on YouTube and sent me a message introducing himself. I was just surfing the internet one day and saw that I had a new notification on my MySpace page. Little did I know that this one message would soon change my entire life.

When I told my mum about the message, she couldn't believe her ears. I was thrilled and so flattered, but I really didn't know what to think about it. I didn't let myself fantasise that this would lead anywhere right off the bat, because Mum and Dad were sceptical. But after they Googled him they felt a little more confident that he was legitimate. He wanted to call us to introduce himself. Mum gave him her mobile number so they could speak directly first. She says she gave him her mobile number instead of our home number so he couldn't track down our house. It may seem extreme, but she was determined to keep us safe. Shawn and Mum had a short conversation and she learned more about his experience in the business. As it turned out, Shawn was a Grammy-nominated producer and songwriter who had worked with big artists like Missy Elliott, Jay-Z, Chris Brown, and others. It was pretty unbelievable that he was interested in me.

Once Mum felt comfortable that he was for real, I started to get excited. This seemed like a big deal! This wasn't something I'd even considered when I posted my first video online. Mum and I began Skyping with Shawn, so we could see each other as well. I even played a few songs that I had written by myself, and he practically fell off his chair saying, 'What the...? Did you knock a 30-year-old songwriter on his head and put him in your pocket?' This made me so proud.

Shawn invited us to come over to the States for a meeting at his house and studio just outside Washington DC. He thought that if I recorded a couple of songs in his studio, we could then send them to a few record labels and see what happened. It felt so amazing to think about working in a studio and having a demo CD. I started to think about which songs I would want to record and how they would sound... That's me – always thinking, always working!

ALWAYS THINKING,
ALWAYS WORKING

It was a big decision to make the trip at all. It meant flying to the other side of the world to meet someone I'd never met, without being sure how legitimate it all was. We just treated it as an experiment, initially, like a test to see if I had what it takes in the studio. My parents remained sceptical, which was good for me. If they'd allowed me to get ahead of myself and believe that this was the start of something big, I'd have been crushed if it didn't work out. Alli thought it was very cool that an American record producer was calling me, and she wanted to come on the trip too, but my parents didn't want to take her out of school.

That was in September 2009. Dad and I flew from Brisbane to Los Angeles, then from LA to DC. It was my first trip out of the country. I had travelled a bit with my swimming club, and we'd flown a few times to different meets around Australia. But this was the furthest I'd ever been! We didn't travel much or take a lot of family vacations when I was a kid. We couldn't afford it. Instead, we would take cheaper holidays and we'd

drive for a few hours to beach towns like Noosa and Kingscliff. In any case, why leave when you live in such an idyllic place?

So overall we were pretty excited about the trip. I could hardly stand the anticipation as I counted down the days to our departure. In the last day or two I did my packing, with the help of Mum and Alli, of course. But I really had no idea what to expect. I certainly had never actually considered there being a real future in music for me, but at this point I was starting to dream that it was possible. Although I'm naturally sceptical, and it might have taken me a little longer than the next guy, now it was really starting to feel like this whole new world was opening up for me. And I was thrilled! I was 12 and about to see America for the first time – and setting off on a potentially life-changing journey.

We landed at the airport in Washington DC and Shawn met us there. We went first to Shawn's house in Maryland to record in his studio there. He had a cool house, in a nice neighbourhood, and having a built-in studio struck me as pretty amazing. I brought some new songs I had written shortly before we left for the States, and some of the older ones I had been working on for a while. We also planned to write some new songs together. The studio was in his basement. I was stoked to get in front of the microphone and put on those big padded headphones for the first time.

I could tell Dad was excited to see me in a professional studio setting. For the very first time it felt real. Shawn was great to work with, and it felt like a natural collaboration from the start. We wrote and recorded for only a few days, and got four pretty good songs from it to use for a demo. Shawn seemed to understand me and my music. He's a really straight-forward guy, and when he said my songs spoke to him, I took it seriously. We posted one of the songs from the demo on YouTube – 'One', which Shawn and I wrote together.

I think we were all surprised at how good the demo sounded! I was used to singing a cappella or just accompanying myself on the guitar. The sound from a proper studio was so much better. With full production my songs sounded like real songs; like ones you'd hear on the radio. And that's when we started really believing that something might actually come out of this.

That said, I tried not to get too far ahead of myself, so that I remained focused on swimming. We tried to fit in a few training sessions in Baltimore while I was over there. It was important to keep in touch with the water and stay in shape while I was away. My swimming coach even arranged for me to meet Michael Phelps. If nothing else were to happen as a result of that trip to the US, at least I got to meet one of my heroes! He was very friendly, and he's such an inspiration – every bit the role model that I had hoped he would be. I'm still embarrassed about asking him to sign ten swimming caps for all my swimming friends back home – doing that during his designated training time must have been incredibly annoying. Sorry, mate!

We planned to take advantage of being on the East Coast, and Shawn drove us up to New York City to introduce us to a few music executives. The meetings went well, but they were short meet-and-greets. I left them with my demo but never played them anything. I didn't know what to expect from these meetings, so I was thrilled when they asked for my demo and seemed interested in meeting me.

It was my first time in New York City. Shawn drove us into the city at night, right into Times Square. All lit up against the dark sky, it was very dreamlike! I was blown away by how many people there were in one place! It was a lot to

Discussing strategy on the phone with my manager.

## I TRIED NOT TO GET TOO FAR AHEAD OF MYSELF

take in: the massive buildings, the bright lights of the big city, the bright yellow taxis I'd seen only in films. Where I'm from is pretty much the exact opposite of Manhattan. There is nothing on the Gold Coast of Australia to prepare you for visiting New York. While we were there, Dad and I also went to a Yankees game. It was the first time I had ever seen baseball!

The whole trip was incredible, and I knew that I wanted to make this opportunity happen. I just kind of fell in love with it — the recording process, the business meetings, the excitement. It wasn't until it actually started happening that it really dawned on me that making music was what I wanted to do -- and that I needed to work hard at it.

# THE WAITING GAME

We went back to Australia – and waited. We were in the States for about two weeks, and the whole trip felt so surreal: recording in a real studio, seeing New York City, and taking meetings with music executives. I decided to record and post a new cover of 'I'm Yours' by Jason Mraz on YouTube. So when I got home, I got to work and channelled all my energy into recording new videos, practising, and writing new songs. The video got something like 200,000 views within the first few weeks. I was shocked! It wasn't that different from any of my previous videos, so I'm not sure why this one went crazy, but it did! I couldn't believe that so many people from around the world watched it. This video also got noticed by record labels, who started to contact me. They said that they loved the videos I posted and they wanted to know more. Even Mike Caren and Chris Morris from Atlantic Records, Jason Mraz's label, contacted me on my YouTube page and asked my parents to contact them for a meeting! Mum also got messages from Sony at the same time! By then I think the record companies were scouting for new talent online because of Justin Bieber and how he was discovered.

Offers from the labels started coming in, and one wanted to sign me on the spot. I was floored! That tiny dream I'd been secretly harbouring since those nights singing along around the barbecue or seeing Keith Urban in concert for the first time could be coming true. But Mum and Dad were naturally wary. We didn't want to rush into anything. And if these labels believed in me like they said they did, well, they would still be there when we were ready. I didn't know what to expect or if anything would come from the trip and recording the demo. So after taking those few weeks off, I threw myself into catching up in school and swimming.

At the same time I started getting serious with music. After all, a career in music wasn't going to happen on its own. I wrote a couple more songs on my guitar and worked much harder at playing and practising regularly, even though I was back at school and swimming training. Though we planned to go back to the States pretty quickly, about a month or two later, for now all we could do was wait.

Keeping up with social media on the Paradise tour.

# REBEL WITH A CAUSE

In junior high school, I developed a great relationship with the music teacher, whose name was Tim Brown. We had a cool connection, and he could see there was something musical in me, even though I never told him about my YouTube videos or the demo. He would sneak me in at lunchtime or before school to record some of my songs, or for extra guitar lessons, and would allow me to rehearse and record in his studio. And sometimes he would invite one of my mates, Lochie O'Keefe, who was a drummer. We played some good covers together, and performed some of them at school talent shows.

The funny thing is that during my last year of school in Australia, I got a C in music. You would think that I could totally nail that class, since I play guitar and sing, and got along well with the music teacher. But because he knew what I was capable of, Mr Brown was always very hard on me – harder than he was on the other students. The class was aimed at beginners, so he focused on the very basics of notes and chords, and general music knowledge. It really didn't seem interesting or educational to me, and I wouldn't always be listening.

I'd always be great at actually doing the assignments and stuff, but in class I'd just sit in the corner and talk to my friends, because I didn't feel like I had much to learn. So he gave me a C, just on effort, or lack thereof. Outside of class, I would be jamming with Mr Brown, so he knew how passionate I was about music. My passion just didn't translate into how I did in his class. I guess sometimes it's not about what you do, but about what you're capable of doing.

In everything else, like maths and science, I got As and A pluses; but a C for music — I mean, what? My mum was like, 'How does this happen?'

Ironically, around the same time I also got kicked out of the school choir. I signed up for it because the teacher knew of my vocal skills and encouraged me to join. I also figured it couldn't hurt to be singing more. Mum thought it would be a good idea too, but I hated being forced into singing one part, and then having to wait around while the teacher worked with the other students. So I goofed off and didn't pay attention, and messed around with my friends instead of singing. And that's how I got kicked out of choir. I never signed up to sing in a group again.

# THE BIG DECISION

A few months after we got back from the States, in December 2009, we heard that a few of the record labels in New York wanted to meet me again. It was so exciting to know that I was still on their radar. So, on 26 December, off we went to New York City and Los Angeles. By this time we had narrowed it down to Sony and Atlantic Records, and we hoped that this round of meetings would help us decide. The whole family went this time, which made it more of a fun trip. We had never been on an overseas holiday together, and we all wanted to go to Disneyland. We spent over a month in the States and got to do a lot more sightseeing this time. My school was excited for me and helped me to get work done while travelling for meetings.

In New York, we stayed in Times Square, right in the heart of the action. We went ice skating at the Rockefeller Center, walked around Central Park, and saw a Broadway show. We went to M&M World there, which Alli and Tom loved. Seeing snow was special, too, as that's something we rarely see in Australia. All the Christmas lights were still up, so it was my first ever glimpse of what it might be like to have a white Christmas.

Left: In the studio, deep in thought. Below: Relaxing and checking texts before showtime.

DURING THE TRIP, I DID A SHOWCASE IN NEW YORK'S TRIBECA NEIGHBOURHOOD. IT WAS MY VERY FIRST PERFORMANCE

We went to meetings with both record labels, where we played my demo for them. I had the meeting with Atlantic Records on my thirteenth birthday, and we were there for hours. One guy would talk to the next guy, and invite us into the next meeting. I had no idea who these people were! They were obviously very successful music executives, but I didn't know enough to be nervous. I really didn't grasp what any of this could mean. Eventually, I got to talk to the co-president of Atlantic Records, Craig Kallman.

I performed for them in these small meetings, all day, as they kept bringing in more and more senior people to meet me. And when I got to the top-level meetings, they also asked if I could dance. When I said yes, I knew I'd have to prove it. So I grabbed a water bottle off the table and used it as a microphone while I showed them some moves. Dad was totally surprised! He had no idea I could dance like that.

During the trip, I did a showcase in New York's Tribeca neighbourhood. It was my very first performance. We just put a showcase together and invited some label executives. I just thought, let's bring out the fans and see who comes. I tweeted out the details of the show and hoped fans would come to support me. I had built enough of a fan base from YouTube for us to get almost 100 people! That was huge for me at the time!

After the East Coast, we spent a few days in Maryland to see Shawn Campbell and record a few more songs with him before we flew to Los Angeles for a few days to take some more meetings. We stayed in West Hollywood and also did some sightseeing, including a visit to Disneyland, which Alli and Tom loved!

It was in LA that we first met Mike Caren, president of A&R for all of Warner Music Group's labels (including Atlantic Records). He invited us to his huge, beautiful house. He's a big deal in the music industry, so we were all excited to be there and, to be honest, I was incredibly nervous. I brought

Above: My mate and road manager Justin Stirling.
Right: Views over Central Park from my hotel.

my guitar and played him a few songs. He said immediately that he loved what I did and thought I could really go places. Of course, now he's a great team-mate and someone I work with regularly on my musical direction.

It took a while for it all to sink in. I hadn't really thought about what it would mean to be a professional musician. I was so focused on swimming, and I was only 13 years old. But after hearing from Shawn, and taking the meetings and getting an offer to sign with a few different record labels, it just felt like an amazing opportunity. I knew that I would regret not seizing it with both hands.

Not surprisingly, my swimming suffered while I was travelling back and forth to the States. We realised eventually that I had to make a decision – music or swimming. Obviously I was heartbroken that I couldn't do both. But ever since being contacted by Shawn and meeting the labels, my head – and heart – had been won over by music. I knew I had to see it through. This was my chance. I love swimming, and it was very difficult to walk away from the dream of swimming for Australia at the Olympics. Some part of me still wonders, what if...? In fact, I think about it a lot, but I don't regret for a minute the choice I made. I know in my heart that I can always go back to swimming in the future because I'm still so young.

We waited a while to make the decision about which label to sign with. It felt important to have a label that was focused on working with me and releasing songs soon. It took a few months for us to decide. It was too important to rush into it, even though the labels were getting a bit antsy. I think they were expecting us just to jump at the chance, but my mum and dad wanted to make sure that I felt comfortable and that they felt comfortable that I would be looked after as a young musician.

Ultimately, it came down to instincts and emotions. Even though Atlantic Records is home to some of the biggest artists in the world – Led Zeppelin, Phil Collins, Jason Mraz, Bruno

Mars, etc. – they felt just like family. My impression was that they would be very involved and that they would do right by me. They were enthusiastic about my music, and they got what I wanted to do. We felt they would encourage me, not just as a singer, but also as a songwriter. Atlantic also said they didn't want to make any changes to what I was already doing – they just wanted to get behind me and my ideas. More than anything, I felt comfortable with them – and ultimately that meant everything.

At first we didn't think we would have to move to the States to do this. We thought I could just work from Australia, but once it actually happened, we all realised we would have to move to Los Angeles or New York City.

That was a tough decision to come to terms with. I had never thought of a future outside Australia. That was where my home, my friends, and my family were. But at the same time, I wanted this chance more than anything I'd ever wanted before. Ultimately it became my parents' decision. They saw that I really wanted to do it, and they knew it was a one in 100 million opportunity. We also knew from the start that we wouldn't split up as a family. If I was moving, we were all moving. My parents hoped that Alli and Tom would see it as their own great adventure, too.

My parents always encouraged me to take every opportunity and live my life to the fullest. A close friend of ours summed it up for my parents by saying: 'How do you say no to your child wanting to chase his dreams? It's what parents do for their kids.' We would have all wound up regretting it if they'd said no. I was (and still am) so grateful that they took the risk. At the end of the day, they said, if it doesn't work out and I don't find success in the music biz, it would still be an adventure. And we can all go back to what we were doing before; at least we'd know we gave it a go and had a fun time doing it. It's something never to be forgotten, and it's a good experience. Given the chance, you have to chase your dreams.

*The*

# Big

## CHAPTER FIVE

## Move

# A PAINFUL GOODBYE

The move to a whole new continent was, of course, a big deal for my family! We were leaving behind all of our family and friends – who were surprised at first. Of course, everyone in our lives knew that I was interested in music and had been recording videos, but few people knew that the conversations with record labels had become so serious. Who imagined that it could all happen so quickly! Our friends and family were absolutely thrilled for me, and for us all to be embarking on this adventure. They were sad to see us go, though, and all of the celebrations were a little sad, too.

It was so hard to say goodbye to everyone that I had grown up seeing every day – from Nanna and Poppa, who would no longer be around the corner, to all our family friends who came over for barbecues every weekend. For my grandma and grandad, who lived just an hour away in Brisbane, and for both my aunties and uncles and all my cousins, it was hard. I realised that this was to be a great sacrifice for all of us.

My last swimming meet was bittersweet. I still won my events – so I got to leave on top! – but it was really difficult finishing my last race not knowing whether I would ever compete again. Telling my coach was even harder. Honestly, I felt really

bad about telling him I was moving to the States and giving up swimming. He was happy for me and respected my decision, but he was disappointed. Even now, Denis is still trying to get me back in the pool. I really didn't like the feeling that I'd let down someone I looked up to and respected. I wasn't telling everyone on the team why I was moving. I just wanted to keep it among close friends and family for the time being.

The year before I moved to the States, I had met a girl who I had a bit of a crush on. I spent all my time in school hanging out with her instead of my friends. It got to the point where a teacher pulled me aside and told me to go and play rugby with the boys and leave her alone! I didn't listen,

IT WAS SO HARD TO SAY GOODBYE TO

of course. She was pretty upset when I told her I was moving to the States and that we had to break it off. It was a very innocent thing, but I was still sad to say goodbye.

I hadn't told a lot of my friends about my YouTube videos and the attention they were getting. I guess that's just who I am. I'm not a guy who likes to brag. I've just always been pretty quiet about everything that I do. In the same way, I didn't even tell my closest friends that I had won six gold medals in swimming. They knew I was a really good swimmer, and that I went to the Nationals, but I didn't tell them how I did or anything. When anyone asked, I'd just tell them something vague like, 'Oh, you know, pretty good.'

RYONE I'D GROWN UP SEEING EVERY DAY

# YOU'VE GOT TO TAKE CHANCES

My friends saw me do the school performances, but they didn't know that I had record labels lining up to sign me. A couple of my closest friends knew that I'd posted videos and that people were watching them, but no one else really had any clue what was going on. They knew I was singing and stuff, but they had no idea of the enormity of the situation. I just told them literally a couple of weeks before I moved to the States – at which point I had to tell them. They were pretty shocked!

That said, I did tell my good swimming mate Jake Thrupp about my trips to the record companies in the US. Then I told him we were thinking about moving to LA, and he was really disappointed, but at the same time really supportive of my decision. We used to see each other for something like four hours a day at our swimming practices, and had become really good friends. Of course, I was going to miss him! I still do. Good friends like that don't come along often.

There were a couple of people, not close friends, who didn't understand what I was doing. They thought I was being pretty crazy for moving to the States to pursue this.

That's okay. There are always going to be a few haters. My feeling is: at the end of the day, you've got to take chances. Otherwise, you'll never know what could happen. I wasn't going to spend the rest of my life wondering 'what if'. My parents taught me this and encouraged me never to listen to negative stuff.

To be fair, Alli didn't really want to move at first. She was happy and didn't want to leave her friends and the rest of our family. She was pretty upset for a while. She cried a lot during our last few weeks on the Gold Coast. That upset me. And I know it was hard for Mum, too. She took a lot of long walks on the beach, crying. Tom was less emotional about the move because he just wasn't old enough to realise the implications. He knew that he'd miss our family and friends, but he was mainly excited about going.

We packed up our house, and when I started packing up my room, I think it really hit me for the first time. We had a couple of big garage sales. Alli and I even sold some of our own stuff and got to keep the profits. Mum taught us how to negotiate to try to get as much money as we could. It was fun actually. We only took the basics and our favourite things with us to LA. We gave our car and the last of the furniture to some family and friends.

We had quite the crew with us at the airport to say goodbye and see us off: my grandparents on both sides; my cousins Rae, Charlie, Billie, Vinnie, Kai, and Ryley; my aunties Nicole and Jodie and uncles Neil and John; and my good mates Jake, Campbell, and Josh. It was very emotional. It seemed like everyone was crying as we hugged goodbye.

We got on the plane – Mum, Dad, Alli, Tom, and I – and we were all thinking our own thoughts, mostly about what and who we would be missing the most, and wondering what was ahead. As our plane took off, I looked out of the window at the city getting smaller underneath us, and the beautiful coastline of Australia. I couldn't imagine what amazing experiences and adventures were awaiting us in Hollywood!

Clockwise from top: Happy ninth birthday, Tommy; hanging with friends Giorgia, Jake, and Alli; chilling with mates on the Gold Coast.

# TOUGH TIMES

When we first arrived in LA, we lived in a hotel in West Hollywood for six months. We had a one-bedroom suite with a fold-out couch in the living room – for our whole family of five. There were enough beds for everyone, obviously, but it was a tight fit, for sure. That said, I think it brought us closer. It was supposed to be that way just until we found a house, but that ended up taking much longer than we thought.

It just got so ridiculous being there for six months that a couple of times, when the hotel was pretty quiet, they let us move to a suite with a kitchenette. It felt like a big upgrade for those few days! Mum would cook on the little stove, and there was more room, so we could spread out a bit. They were doing us a favour, and when the hotel got busy again, we would have to move back to our cramped quarters. We obviously got to know some of the staff pretty well and they remain good friends.

For the time being, the hotel was really our only option. We knew where we wanted to live, but we had no support network there at all, which made it difficult. We had a rental car for most of the time, too. It felt like everything was in transition for a while.

It was pretty solitary and boring back then. Especially for my family. Mum and Dad would take turns coming with

Left: Miami v Lakers with Alli and Jake.
Below: Sibling silliness.

me to meetings or to the studio, while the other hung back and tried to find something to do with Alli and Tom. Usually there wasn't much going on – just a trip to the grocery store or something simple like that. They also spent a lot of time on Skype talking to our friends and family back in Australia.

Alli was 12 when we moved to Los Angeles and I think we all agree it was hardest for her. She was a very popular and social girl in Australia, so it was really difficult for her to be this isolated. Alli talked to her friends a lot during our first few months and it took a while for her to meet new friends and warm up to Los Angeles. I knew she was missing our old life. But she didn't like to let me see her upset. When I did, it would just hit me hard. I worried a lot about her, and all of them. Now she's happy, has a blossoming career of her own, and lots of friends. I think she loves Los Angeles now. But those first couple of months were really tough. I felt responsible. I used to apologise to Alli a lot. She would reassure me that we were all in it together. After all, that's what family is for. Alli's support meant the world to me, and it still does.

# INTO THE STUDIO

For my part, I went straight into the studio when I arrived in LA. That's where I stayed for the first month – writing, recording, and perfecting my first singles and the first EP. Some nights I'd be there until 3 a.m. – pretty late for a 13-year-old. Sometimes I couldn't even keep my eyes open, but I loved the process so much and I never wanted to leave. We all knew it was time to go when I fell asleep. Swimming had taught me all about working hard and pushing myself to achieve my goals.

Of course, it helped that I loved what I was doing! It was my first time in a real recording studio. When I had recorded my demo during my first trip to the States, I had worked in a home studio in Shawn's house. This felt like I'd really made it to the big league.

I spent a lot of time in the studio observing and learning everything that was going on around me, asking questions of the sound mixers, engineers, and techs. Shawn Campbell was there producing some tracks, and I also worked with songwriter/producer and artist Lil' Eddie. He's written songs for some amazing artists, including Usher, Janet Jackson, Pink, Nelly Furtado, and Jessie J. Plus he's a vocal coach on the American *X Factor*. I completed something like 13 songs

# I LOVED GETTING INTO THE STUDIO

during those studio sessions with Lil' Eddie, including 'All Day'. Some of them made it onto my first EP, *4U*, but a lot of them never came out.

I focused a lot on learning the production side so that I would be able to deliver what the song needed. I wanted to learn everything. I was a sponge, really. And now I'm much more independent when it comes to writing music and shaping my sound.

It paid off pretty quickly. I learned enough to be able to move on to the next song and always keep the pace going. That's a point of pride for me. I'm working with such amazing professionals; I want to make sure I'm professional, too. I worked hard and paid attention to everything so I could do it better the next time.

# STAYING CONNECTED

In those first few weeks and months in Los Angeles, I was thrilled to be pursuing this amazing opportunity, and working hard – but I couldn't help worrying about what I'd got my family into. Of course, it was my parents' decision to move us all to the States, but I was the reason. And before things really started happening for me, I kept asking myself: 'What have I led us all into?'

Tom had the weirdest transition, to me anyway. He has never really experienced school, as we left when he was in first grade and we've been taught by a tutor ever since we moved to LA. I just hoped that he would find his interests and make his own friends. It's hard moving halfway around the world when you're so young. I hoped he wasn't missing out. The bottom line was that Tom and Alli weren't moving for themselves. They both love it in LA now, but that took a while. Recently Tom has said he feels really lucky that he gets to travel so much and see the world, and hates the idea of a real school, which has made me feel better about everything. I know that taking the leap and moving was the right decision.

We're all thriving in our own ways now, and the move has brought us closer as a family. We grew very close while living in that hotel for six months, not knowing anyone else when we moved here, and it's been our experiences since then that have made us the family we are.

We go home to Australia enough to feel connected, at least twice a year. But what's hardest for me is hearing about my friends back home surfing every day, going to parties, and hanging out with girls. I moved to Los Angeles before I went to high school. I didn't get to experience a lot of the normal teenager stuff. Plus, of course, I think about swimming a lot. So many of my mates and family friends are involved in swimming, and some of them have started to reach elite levels and make the Olympic teams in Australia. My family and I root for them, of course, but sometimes I get a little nostalgic and wistful. I can't help feeling I want to be there, too. But I can't do both, and I'm happy where I am. I've done things that I never would have dreamed possible. How can I not love my life?

Staying connected to our friends and family back home is a major priority for all of us. When things started going well for me, my parents didn't focus on new luxuries or buying anything extravagant. Instead, Alli and I got to invite friends over to Los Angeles for visits. We would each pick one friend, buy their tickets, and they would fly over together so they had company. My parents always said this was the best luxury we could buy.

We felt like we could still have our friends in our life and still have a bit of home with us. It's the best of all worlds, and we try to make it happen whenever we can.

Above: With friends and family back on the Gold Coast. Right: Chill times in the Bahamas.

## CHAPTER SIX

# From Surf Waves to Radio Waves

# IYIYI

In March 2010, three months before we moved to the States, Dad and I had come to Los Angeles for more meetings with Atlantic and to record my first single: 'iYiYi', featuring Flo Rida. We released the single in June 2010, the same time we moved to States.

'iYiYi' is still one of my biggest hits and something I'll probably always be known for. I was a big Flo Rida fan and was completely ecstatic to have him contribute to the song. I couldn't believe that someone I listened to myself, and who had major hits on the radio, was going to be on my song. The funny thing is that he had actually heard the beat before I recorded the song and wanted it for himself. We share the same A&R man at Atlantic, Mike Caren, and I basically said, 'Mike, tell him that it's my song and it's going to be my single, but he can do a verse.' Mike laughed and thought I had some real bravado to say that. But you know what, Flo Rida agreed – and the song was a hit, going gold in several countries, including Australia and Canada!

I thought it was a pretty catchy tune. Alli thought it was a really good song and that it sounded good for my voice. I trust her taste in music, so I was psyched to have her stamp of approval.

Making the 'iYiYi' video.

The majority of the video was filmed on the Gold Coast before we moved to LA, and it really showed my normal beach-town life in a way. It showed me riding bikes, skateboarding, and hanging out on the beach with a crew of my friends. And obviously I'm professing my feelings for a very beautiful girl. It was so unbelievable to film a real music video! It felt a little odd to be performing in front of the cameras at first, but then I really just had fun with it. Filming my first music video gave me my first taste of what being a recording artist was all about.

The first time I heard the song on the radio I was in Louisville, Kentucky, having dinner with the programme director of the radio station there. He said, 'Come outside. I want you to hear something.' He turned on the radio station in his car and 'iYiYi' started playing. We had it blasting on the side road. It was on right after a Katy Perry song. It was one of those amazing moments that make you take a step back and think, 'Wow, this is really happening!' After it ended, I just sat there in shock for, like, half an hour, thinking about how I'm 13 and I have a song on the radio with Flo Rida. Listening and looking back on the 'iYiYi' days of my career, I can't help thinking how young I look and sound, and how much I've improved since then. We've all got to start somewhere, though, eh?!

'iYiYi' hit the Top Five at Radio Disney and was in three different charts for 19 weeks in total. It peaked at number 19 on the Australia Singles Top 50, where it stayed for two weeks. To date, the music video has had more than 23 million views! It was a milestone for me at the time. To have such a positive response to my first single gave me the momentum to think about the next one and about releasing an EP that my fans would really love. My fan base was growing, it seemed, and I began to feel the love on my website, Twitter, Facebook, and, of course, on YouTube.

# 4U

My first EP was called *4U* and it came out in December 2010. I had worked hard on it under some pretty hectic conditions following the move to the States. The EP featured some of the best music I'd recorded at the time: 'iYiYi', 'All Day', 'Round of Applause', 'Don't Cry Your Heart Out', and an acoustic version of 'iYiYi'.

We did a photo shoot for the cover, and for publicity stills. It was one of my first photo shoots, so I tried to follow the photographer's directions and look my best. I didn't have much to say creatively, whereas now I really control everything I put out. I was just new to the situation — to my whole career. I'm just glad the EP cover came out looking so slick, even though I didn't have much idea of what I was doing at the time!

I was stoked to get *4U* out there to see what the fans would think! It felt like my true test. The response to the EP turned out to be phenomenal! It spent six weeks on Billboard's Canadian Hot 100 chart, and within the first couple of weeks after releasing the music video it had already hit one million views on YouTube.

The *4U* EP went to number two on iTunes Australia, and was number four on the Billboard Heatseekers Albums list.

MY FAMILY
AND I WERE
KIND OF
STUNNED BY
THE SUCCESS
OF THE EP

My family and I were kind of stunned by the success of the EP. It was surreal seeing my name in the charts next to some of the artists I had grown up listening to and admiring. To my friends and family back home I think it was the first affirmation that perhaps we had made the right decision in moving to the US. To me it felt like the journey was beginning in earnest and it made me hungry for more.

# TOURING WITH GREYSON

Shortly after the EP came out, I embarked on a co-headline tour with Greyson Chance in the spring of 2011. We played all across the US, from New York City to Fort Lauderdale, from Dallas to Seattle. They were all fairly small venues, and it was a thrill to see packed houses. It was my first experience where I had a lot of fans coming out and singing along. I was feeding off the fans' energy and having the raddest time.

Greyson plays the piano, and got his start by posting a video of himself playing Lady Gaga's 'Paparazzi' at a school talent show – kind of like I did. At the time, we were in sort of the same spot in our careers and we were experiencing life on the road for the first time. I think having that connection made our life on the road a bit more enjoyable. Alli and Greyson hit it off immediately and they became close friends.

We shared a bus for six weeks and talked about music quite a bit. We didn't have too many days off. We liked it that way. During the tour, I was always writing and composing songs. I kept working, thinking about my next project.

That was when my voice changed. A couple of times during the 4U and Coast to Coast tours my voice cracked while I was onstage. It was so embarrassing. I tried to make

**Touring with Greyson Chance.**

a joke of it. I was like, 'Oh sorry, it's just puberty.' That usually got a good laugh, but it was still really embarrassing.

That period was really difficult for me. I started taking more intense voice lessons to help me through it and to help me protect my voice as it changed. We had to pitch down some songs in order for me to be able to perform them. Only recently have I felt that my voice has started to settle into my adult range. The hardest part has been getting my falsetto to a point that I am happy with. I know puberty comes with its ups and downs, but it's been a lot harder for me going through it in front of an audience!

# CHAPTER SEVEN

## My
## Music
## Family

# MY BIG BROTHER

In August 2011, my parents and I decided to bring in Matt Graham and Scooter Braun to help us navigate the next chapter in my career. Scooter Braun is a talent manager who represents Justin Bieber, PSY, Carly Rae Jepsen, Asher Roth, and The Wanted. So it was incredible that he was really interested in helping take me to the next level. As part of this, he introduced me to Matt, whom he had known since their college years at Emory together. We knew that music had become a young man's game, particularly in pop music, since it's so much about social media. Matt and Scooter were in college when Facebook came out. They are basically the oldest people who grew up with social media. It makes sense that they are masters of it.

Matt is 13 years older than I am, which is the same age difference as between Justin and Scooter. Matt was young but had been in management with other acts for several years, and I could tell he was really bright and hungry to prove himself in the industry. When we first met, we hit it off immediately. Matt appreciated that I had a clear sense of who I am as an artist, and he totally got behind me. He felt that I had the tools needed to do big things, but that I needed someone to guide me. And my parents, well, they wanted

BEFORE LONG, MATT
BECAME A BONA FIDE
PART OF THE FAMILY

someone around every day that we really trusted and who they believed would be a great mentor. And that was Matt.

Before long, Matt became a bona fide part of the family, often living at our house when he needed to come to LA. I feel like he gets me, and he's just fun to be around. He's a good influence and keeps me on a straight path. I spend a lot of time with him, and my parents really trust him, which is so important to me. My dad and Matt are also pretty close. Age-wise, Matt is right between me and my parents, which means he sometimes bridges the gap there. We also have very similar music tastes, which is a great advantage and helps shape my vision for where I'm going with my career – we've even written a few songs together. We have similar goals when it comes to proving ourselves in the music industry, and we're both extremely keen to achieve success and leave our mark on the world. Our similarity in motivation and work ethic has made us great partners.

We recently celebrated his wife Sarah's birthday at a barbecue at their new house in LA. Sarah is brilliant. She's just really warm and wonderful. I was pretty thrilled that she wanted to spend her birthday with me and my family. She's a lawyer and super intelligent. She moved to LA from New York and, at a time when next to no one was hiring, she got five job offers from the five biggest firms here. Quite impressive. She moved here to be with Matt, who came here to be with me, actually. So I'm always extra nice to Sarah, since I was the cause of all this commotion.

**Right: G'Day LA Gala with Matt and Alli.**

Scooter's company is one of the most successful in the business right now, so he is busy making deals happen for all of the artists that his company looks after. Scooter and I talk on the phone often; he joins us for a lot of the important stuff, and the three of us often get together to discuss the big-picture strategy for my career.

But my relationship with Matt is so much deeper than just business. Even if I quit today (which I won't!), I would still go over to Matt's to crash. Even 10 or 20 years from now, I know I'll still be good mates with him. I think that illustrates the kind of relationship we have. I talk to him about everything and he gives me advice and helps me out with a lot of things relating to my career as well as my personal life. It's pretty amazing to be in business with a guy who's basically the big brother I never had.

# COAST TO COAST

After coming off the tour with Greyson Chance, I went back into the studio to finish writing and recording some songs for my next EP, which I decided to call *Coast to Coast*. I wanted a name that reflected my journey from the Gold Coast to the California coast. It was such a huge move for me and my family, and I wanted the name of the EP to reflect the experience – as a sort of thank-you for everything they've done and sacrificed. *Coast to Coast* featured six songs, including a few hits like 'All Day', 'Angel', and 'On My Mind'.

I think my music evolved from 'iYiYi' to *Coast to Coast*. The new EP was way more mature. The songs have more meaning. I think they reflect my life and, given the way my fans have reacted, I think – I hope! – anyone can relate to them.

Mike Caren, Pete Ganbarg, and their Atlantic Records A&R team, which includes Chris Morris and Aaron Bay-Schuck, trusted my instincts and helped me to shape my sound, to determine who I am as an artist. Mike really values my opinion, which is flattering given his achievements in music. Because of my age, I think most people in the industry wouldn't trust me the way he does. And it goes both ways. I have learned to trust his instincts musically as well, and I think the record was so much better for it.

# COAST TO COAST WAS A THANK YOU TO MY FAMILY FOR EVERYTHING THEY'VE DONE AND SACRIFICED

Feeling pretty messy
after a show.

But getting to that point took a lot of work. In the beginning, it was difficult for me to trust him on a song that I didn't immediately gravitate towards. If he played me a song and I didn't like it right off the bat, I wouldn't want to record it. But Mike was smart – and persistent. He'd encourage me just to try it, to put my own spin on it. And inevitably, once I did, once I found a way to make it my own, I would end up loving it!

That happened with 'Not Just You'. To be honest, I didn't like that song at first. But Mike told me just to go in and record it. He brought in a very talented songwriter and Grammy-award-winning producer named Nasri Atweh to help with it. Nasri pushed me on this song, and as a result of our work together he's now one of my favourite songwriters to work with. So I learned to really trust Mike. He is one of the reasons I'm thankful I signed with Atlantic.

Before *Coast to Coast* came out, I asked Alli for her opinion on a few songs. She's the same age as my fans and I trust her. She really connected to 'Crazy But True' and 'Good As It Gets'. That she responded so strongly to those tracks made me feel much more confident about releasing the EP. She's my sister. I know she'll always tell me the truth, no matter what.

This EP also shows the two types of music that I'm most drawn to and inspired to create: funky up-tempo tracks like 'Good As It Gets', and songs with a beachy, acoustic vibe like 'Angel', which is guitar-driven but laid-back and insanely catchy.

*Coast to Coast* really reflects who I am as an artist, so it's an important EP for me. Even if it hadn't been a success, I'd have been proud of it for that reason. But, luckily, my fans loved it. It debuted at number 12 on the Billboard Top 200 Albums chart and two of the songs on the CD went to number one on Radio Disney. I was pretty stoked and felt truly validated as an artist.

# VIDEO STAR

With *Coast to Coast*, I had the opportunity to make music videos for a few of the singles. These videos were on a whole different scale from anything I'd done before. They explored what the song was about and were meant to really draw fans in.

I'm very involved in all my videos, especially in the initial concept for them. I start by thinking of how I can expand on the meaning of the song. A song can tell you a lot and I feel like you can really emphasise and magnify its meaning in a video. The video for 'On My Mind' was the first one where I really took the lead in creating the concept. We shot it at the Topanga Mall in Los Angeles. It blew me away when I went to the mall to discover that they'd closed all the shops so I could film.

I felt like a lot of guys my age could relate to the concept of the video. The idea is that I see a beautiful girl and I want to find out who she is, so I run through the mall and talk to people to try to find her. I think we've all wished we could do that at some time. I like the fact that it ends positively, with us finally meeting.

I LOVE SINGING
SLOW SONGS;
IT'S A CHANCE
TO REALLY
EMBRACE THE
VOCALS AND
EMOTION

Serenading my Angels.

Of all the music videos I've done, 'Not Just You' is one of my favourites. It shows a more mature and emotional side of me. I collaborated with an amazing director named Roman White, and he really pushed me to act in this one. We filmed on Venice Beach and in downtown LA. The video shows a girl who got away, and I beg her not to leave me. I'm trying to make it back to her, chasing her, trying to get her back before it's too late. It was the first time I'd really been held up as a romantic lead. It was my first big ballad. I love singing slow songs like that; it's a chance to really embrace the vocals and emotion. I think I've made a few girls' nights over the past year or so by bringing them up onstage and singing them that song.

That was a real step forward for me creatively, to be able to pull off this emotional song and act well enough in the video. I was really proud of what we'd done. It was the first one I'd done where I didn't want to change anything after I'd watched it all the way through. I think we got this one right.

Onstage, I feel right at home.

# FAN FEVER

In keeping with the theme of the 'On My Mind' video, I went on the Coast to Coast tour in August 2011, visiting malls across the country and attracting thousands of people to each appearance.

At each mall there were girls everywhere. It was pretty hectic! Five thousand people turned up to the show in Detroit. I think people were surprised that I could attract that kind of crowd, but I love being the underdog. I'd rather be underestimated than overrated. I think Mum and Alli got a kick out of seeing all the girls chanting my name when I walked out onstage.

This was the first time I really got a sense of being famous. I shut down the mall in Sydney. Five thousand showed up in Melbourne. A crowd like that just looked insane. That's a lot of people in a mall.

That tour was overwhelming, but also extremely exciting. For the first time, I took a step back and thought to myself, 'Wow, I'm 14, but this is really happening and it's happening very fast.' I got the sense that this could be real, like my life was changing, like I was making it. It was incredible to see how many people were turning up, and how many were

Feeling the love on the Believe tour.

starting to interact with me on Twitter and Facebook. I hit a million followers on that tour. My fans became so engaged, so active; the Angels, as I like to call them, were growing in number and it was very cool.

Of course, this meant that I started to get recognised, which felt really strange. I am still naturally very shy. I found it difficult to be in front of big groups. On stage, it's like the performance itself helps to distract me from my nerves, but one-on-one it's different. I've had to learn to be more confident and natural. The problem is that when you're a little insecure or shy, it can come off as arrogance. That's so not what I'm about. I'm just mellow.

I remember once, I was with Mum and Alli at the supermarket, and Mum whispered to me, 'There are, like, 20 people over there looking at you.' I was totally oblivious to it at first. Then I saw this swarm of girls following me from aisle to aisle. My mum thought it was hilarious and started filming it – me looking on the shelf and this group of fans sneaking behind each row to get closer. Then, at one point, I was trying to choose some cereal. And there was one girl at one end of the aisle, and another one at the other end, watching. They had me surrounded! It was one of those times when you realise you can't just shop for cereal or pick your nose. People are always watching! Ha!

Fans go up to Alli all the time and ask her weird personal questions about me, like what kind of toothpaste or deodorant I use. It's flattering that fans care so much, but I do try to keep some mystery to what I do. Of course, she understands perfectly what it's like to be a fan. She cried when we arranged for her to meet the Jonas Brothers a few years back!

It's also weird, but kind of awesome, to go into Hollister or Abercrombie & Fitch and hear my song playing on the radio. I walk in and no one knows they're listening to me. I just try to keep calm, smile to myself, and see if anyone's clearly grooving to my music. It's those kinds of small moments that actually mean a lot.

# ELLEN

Being around adults a lot and being in a work environment, I grew up pretty quickly. I've had to stand up for myself and assert myself in business meetings when I'm the youngest person in the room by 15 to 20 years or more. I realise it most when I'm around my best mates. I sometimes feel so mature. Even so, doing media and being interviewed has always been tough for me. I just don't like to talk about myself. It's weird!

The performances on TV are especially nerve-wracking. The cameras make me anxious. I feel like they focus in on every little thing. Plus, usually there are no fans. It feels like I'm singing and dancing for the camera guy. I definitely need to be in front of an audience to get my best energy.

When I got invited to be on *Ellen* for the first time in September 2011, I was super excited. I'm a huge fan of hers and we watch the show all the time as a family. I've also seen how important performing on her show can be for an artist. It's a career milestone.

The interview went well. Matt thought I seemed cool and comfortable – and even funny! However, once it came time to perform, I got incredibly nervous. I never told this to anyone aside from my family and Matt, but I had to redo my

# THE PERFORMANCES ON TV ARE ESPECIALLY NERVE-WRACKING

performance because I messed up the dance. I had learned it only the day before, and I thought I had it down, but I was so nervous, I got tripped up. Ellen was cool about it, but how embarrassing!

Being on *Ellen* was totally surreal. Having seen a lot of other major musicians perform on it, to be on it myself was definitely an unbelievable moment. The whole family was in shock about it. Tom was backstage playing ping pong with Kevin Dillon, an actor from HBO's *Entourage*. It was one of those moments that I'll treasure forever.

CHAPTER EIGHT

# MY HOMECOMING

In October 2010 we had gone back to Australia for the Kids' Choice Awards in Sydney, and I performed 'iYiYi' to close the show, which marked my first performance in Australia. I won the award for 'Fresh Aussie Muso', and the whole crowd was so stoked. It was my first award in music and I just felt really validated. It was a feeling I recognised from swimming. Accepting the award onstage in front of that huge crowd felt a whole lot like stepping up onto that centre block on the awards podium after a race and accepting a medal. It was also the first time I really felt love from my home country. It was a big moment for me, and for my family, to be embraced in Australia. The reality of my success was really starting to sink in.

It was my return to the Aussie KCAs in 2011, though, that truly felt like a homecoming. This time, I performed two songs, presented, and won three awards: the Superfresh Award, the Fave Aussie Muso Award, and the Awesome Aussie Award. Plus, I got totally slimed!

A lot of family and friends came to see us and to support me – grandparents, cousins, aunts and uncles, and quite a few of our closest friends: the Baildons, Thrupps, McCarthys, Greens, Winningtons, Carsleys, and Harrisons. They got a

kick out of seeing me onstage and the whole event. Also, my mates Jake Thrupp, Giorgia Green, Campbell Carsley, and Josh Winnington were there. We made it into a bit of a holiday. We were in Sydney for five days and we all stayed in the same hotel, so we really got to spend time together.

After my second time at the Kids' Choice Awards, I realised how much my life had changed. Hearing about what my mates were up to at school and swimming – the life that I would have been living if I hadn't made the move – made me appreciate how far I'd come. I was glad that my family and friends were able to see first hand what was going on, too. It was easy to say that things were getting crazy in the States, but until they saw it for themselves, they never really understood what I was talking about. Needless to say, they were thrilled for me that the sacrifice had paid off. When it was time to return to the States once more, it was hard to say goodbye to everyone again, but this time when I left I was surer than ever that I had made the right decision.

# KONICHIWA JAPAN!

Right after our amazing trip to Australia, instead of heading straight back to LA we flew to Japan for a few TV and mall performances there. And what a great experience that was!

Before we arrived, my family and I thought nobody would really know me there. We were completely wrong! I got off the plane to hundreds of people waiting in the airport for us to come out. They were holding signs saying things like 'We love you, Cody!' We knew then that the trip was going to be an exciting one. It was crazy seeing people from different countries go wild for me.

My Japanese fans were so polite and respectful. It was my first time visiting another country with such a different culture – and a different language. I had translators with me on the trip. It was awesome seeing fans singing along – especially since English isn't their first language. It just shows how universal music is! I also did a few TV appearances and record label events.

We had the opportunity to do a bit of sightseeing, so we took the bullet train to Kyoto, Osaka, and Tokyo. Everywhere we stopped there were hundreds of fans waiting. It was quite an experience.

Japan! I love you!

Tom liked the trip a lot. He loved the sights and the food there. And I especially loved seeing the temples in Kyoto. I took so many pictures of everything we saw. It was a special time for the family – and a great way to meet so many new fans!

MY PARENTS DON'T
TREAT ME DIFFERENTLY
– I STILL HAVE TO
CLEAN MY ROOM AND
PULL MY WEIGHT
AROUND THE HOUSE

## MY RESPONSIBILITY

Recently, I started to realise that with success comes responsibility. I know that my fans watch what I'm doing so closely. I don't ever want to be perceived as a bad influence. I've always believed that it's important to do the right thing rather than the easy thing.

At home, I don't get in trouble often. I really don't like to upset my parents. They don't treat me any differently – I still have to clean my room and pull my weight around the house. Sometimes I'm tempted to rebel a little, but it's just not worth it. When I see them upset, I really don't feel good at all. I do crave a little bit of freedom, though. That's what I miss most about Australia – I wish I could just go to a friend's place, or go to the mall with a girl. But now that my parents have come to trust a few of our team members on the road, I am getting a lot more freedom.

I definitely feel a big sense of responsibility not to do anything that would disappoint my family, because I'm starting to live a very public life. And the media and fans are starting to become more and more interested in things other than my music.

Alli, too, has started to build her own following through modelling and writing her blog. She has over a million followers on Twitter now. Girls really look up to her. We both need to act the part. Neither of us has all the answers, or even most of the answers for that matter. We're still growing up, learning to find our way, and making mistakes, but that's part of why I think our fans feel so attached to us. We are all figuring it out together.

I think that my relationship with Alli shows that you have to treat siblings with kindness. I get messages all the time saying things like, 'I wish my brother and I or my sister and I could have a friendship like you guys do,' or just 'You guys always look so happy together.' I hope we inspire other siblings to treat each other well. As my parents always say, 'Friendships may come and go, but you'll always have your sibling in your life.'

From left: Doing dishes; posing with my mum; red carpet with my sister Alli; baby pics of my siblings and me with our mum.

# BEATING THE BULLIES

In December 2011, following some rewarding work with the anti-bullying organisation Defeat the Label, I was invited to appear on an episode of *Extreme Makeover: Home Edition* where the crew, led by Ty Pennington, was building a new home for a family who had been deeply affected by bullying. It's really important to me to support the anti-bullying movement, since it's something that affects my fans all over the world.

Being on the show was an eye-opening experience. The house being knocked down was where their youngest son had committed suicide because he couldn't take the bullying any longer. I couldn't even begin to imagine the pain of what they'd been through. Over the years, I've done work on behalf of several anti-bullying organisations, but still it was crazy and heart-breaking to see that it can get that severe and how it can affect an entire family.

# IT'S PRETTY INCREDIBLE TO REALISE THE SORT OF INFLUENCE I CAN HAVE IN THE WORLD

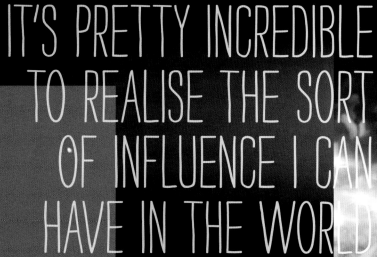

Left: Performing on the Paradise tour.
Right: Performing on the Believe tour.

I get messages about bullying and the *Extreme Makeover* show all the time. They say things like, 'You've given me more confidence. You've given me the strength not to take it so personally.'

So many people get bullied. A lot of people don't realise that, because often victims don't want to tell anyone about it. I've received letters and emails with stories of kids who have been bullied, saying that I helped in some way. It's pretty incredible to realise the sort of influence I can have in the world.

If through my music I can help just one person, then I know I've done something great with my life. Beating the bullies is so much more important to me than any bestselling record, so it's pretty great when I have the chance to do something this important.

# CHAPTER NINE

# My
# Not-So-
# Glamorous
## Hollywood
# Life

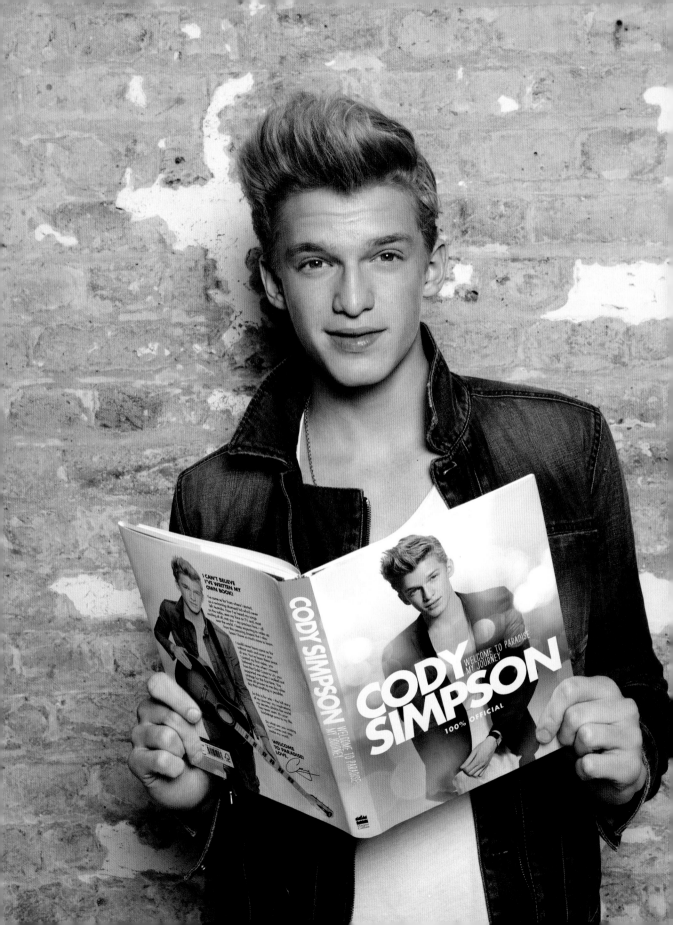

# SCHOOL DAYS

Since I moved to LA, I've been home schooled. I've had 30 different teachers over the past few years, but right now I'm working with a woman named Laura Inman, from Atlanta Country Day School, and she's rad. It's turned out to be much better for me this way. My schedule is crazy, and I've always felt I would rather be outside the classroom pursuing my passions like swimming and music. I do enjoy some of my classes, like English and writing – I'm not especially fond of science – but I never liked the pressurised work in traditional school, or a lot of the cliquey social dynamics there.

Between school, rehearsals, and recording for the new album, it's been a challenge to balance everything I need to get done. Despite that, as with so many other things in my life, I have been working hard and I plan to finish high school early – hopefully before I turn 17. I've been working tirelessly hard to get all my requirements done. It's a hectic schedule, though. I wake up in time for school, which is from 9 a.m. to 12.30 p.m. And then I head straight to the studio, where I usually stay until 7 p.m. After that I'll come home and eat dinner with my family. At other times, before a major tour, I go to dance rehearsals or meetings for tour or album promotions instead of recording in the studio. If I have homework, I do it after that. It's crazy, I know, but it's my life, and I love it regardless of the challenges.

I try to have fun wherever I go. I bring my skateboard to the studio and even though I'm working hard, I keep it light and buy time to do some skating around. Sometimes I have a little too much fun during home-school hours. Tom, Alli, and I have school together and sometimes, I'll admit, I can be a little bit of a distraction. I like to goof off. And I usually do that by singing. A lot. Repetitively. Which always annoys Alli. So our teacher has learned to separate us, and schedule it so I'm distracting Tom and Alli the least. Alli and I have school in the morning, and I often have to move to sit in the kitchen to let her concentrate. Tom has school in the afternoon, since he's at a different grade level.

I know it sounds busy, but back in Australia I would be swimming in the morning for two hours, then at school all day, and then back to swimming training in the afternoon for two hours. Plus two or three hours of homework at night, so I'm used to the long days. I would have weekends and time to hang out with friends, but it was still pretty busy. In some ways, I know that no matter what I'm pursuing – be it music or swimming, or something else entirely – I'm always going to be working hard. It's part of who I am.

That's not to say I don't have fun. The social life in LA is just different. I'm honestly not a big fan of the Hollywood scene. At first I tried to make new friends, but soon realised I'm not interested in being part of any scene and that I just want to focus on my music. I have a few good mates in the US, but I definitely still rely on my mates back home.

IT'S IMPORTANT TO ME TO STAY AS CLOSE AS I CAN TO MY ROOTS ON THE GOLD COAST

It's important to me to stay as close as I can to my roots on the Gold Coast. With my friends back home I can just surf and be who I really am. They keep me grounded and grateful. Back on the Gold Coast, everyone's door was always open. I could pretty much walk to all of my friends' houses, and my mum would let me spend the night here and there. Their mums would always welcome us and have food out. It was a genuine community. I miss that. Los Angeles is huge and just doesn't have that small, surf-town feel.

Sometimes I find it difficult to know who to trust. There have been times when I've realised that girls – ones I thought were great and real and into me – just like me for the wrong reasons. So I don't really make a lot of new friends.

My mum and dad only have a few close friends here, too. They're the same as me. I guess we're all focused on keeping in touch with the people from home.

My mum always says that if I have enough success, I will be able to live wherever I want, which might mean someday being back on the Gold Coast. Maybe I'll end up going back and forth between Los Angeles and Australia. I could have a studio back home. I assume Mum and Dad will move back eventually when I'm old enough to be independent. I assume that Alli will spend more time in LA as well, as she focuses on her career. I'm not sure if that's what Tom will do, because when I'm 20 he'll still be 13. We'll have to see about that. We're just taking it one step at a time, together.

Clockwise from top: Skating with friends Ryan, Harry, and Ryan; chilling on the Gold Coast; hanging with Ryan Nassif.

It's funny – I never went to school dances or proms back home, but I have my own sort of events to look forward to here, like the Grammys, the Kids' Choice Awards, or Justin Bieber's eighteenth birthday party. Now that was a really fun night! Scooter threw Justin a party for his eighteenth in March 2012 at the Beverly Wilshire Hotel. There were a lot of cool people there, including my mates Kendall and Kylie Jenner, Kim Kardashian, Tyler The Creator, Jaden Smith, Selena Gomez, and even Mike Tyson. Justin's grandparents and some child-hood friends also flew in from Canada for the party, which seemed to mean a lot to him. Carly Rae Jepsen sang her big hit, 'Call Me Maybe'. I must admit, we partied pretty hard.

So I don't feel like I'm missing out at all, because I'm getting to have these amazing experiences, with these amazing, talented people. I know I'm lucky. I know I'm blessed. Sure, it'd be fun to go to a prom, but I wouldn't trade my life for anything.

Events like the Grammys are always a good time. Usually, I'll gear up by spending the afternoon picking out my outfit and I'll take a bit longer to get my hair just right. When I get dropped off at the event and step out of the car onto the red carpet, there are fans behind a gate, yelling, paparazzi flashing their cameras, and journalists shouting their questions. It's a pretty sweet feeling. You really feel famous when you're on the red carpet. I don't feel famous day to day, at home or in the studio. It's just not natural to me to feel that way. But when I'm on the red carpet, with all those cameras and fans around, I feel part of that world.

And I love the attention. I absolutely embrace getting recognised. It would be scarier if I wasn't. I like to know my hard work is paying off, and my music is connecting to more and more fans. If I didn't want that, I'd be surfing at home.

# FAMOUS FRIENDS

Alli is my best friend, but of course I do have a few others in LA. Justin Bieber has been a really supportive mate. We've spent nights in the studio, nights chilling in Vegas, Paris, and LA, and he has given me the great opportunity of travelling around the US and the world with him on his Believe tour.

Alli and I also have a great friend in Jessica Jarrell, the R&B/pop singer, and we have spent a lot of time over the last year with Kylie and Kendall Jenner. I am really good mates with Kylie, who is a great confidante. And her whole family was very supportive when I released *Paradise*. In fact, one of my favourite holiday memories was being invited to their big annual Christmas Eve party in 2011. They were so friendly and welcoming, we had a great evening. Because of our busy schedules, hanging out together has been more difficult over the past year, but it's always fun when we can find time.

THEY WERE SO FRIENDLY
AND WELCOMING, WE
HAD A GREAT EVENING

Living legend Roger Daltrey of The Who trying to mess up my hair after our interview together for Teen Cancer America!

Dad and I meeting Lionel Richie.

Below: Serenading my ultimate crush, Miranda Kerr. Top right: Hanging with John Travolta at the G'Day Gala. Bottom right: I'd like to believe Katy Perry was into me that night.

# GIRLS, GIRLS, GIRLS

When it comes to dating, I'm basically a regular teenage guy. I just try to keep it a little more private than most. I'm young and still figuring it all out. In this business it's hard to make a relationship work. Travelling as much as I do puts a strain on it, and it's difficult for a relationship to grow when it happens in the public eye. I don't like holding hands or PDAs (public displays of affection), because I feel like someone is always watching – and taking pictures.

What's my type? I'm usually into girls who are of the wholesome, girl-next-door type. I like a girl with class and self-respect, and a girl that I can trust, as it's difficult for me to find people I can truly talk to about everything. Knowing that my personal thoughts and feelings are safe with them is essential. Trust and honesty are vitally important when it comes to relationships.

I'd honestly like to get married and have kids one day, but not more than three. I'd love to have a house in LA and a house in Australia, and I'd like my kids to be raised where I was – on the Gold Coast.

I'm also a regular teenage guy in a lot of other ways. I have some terrible habits that annoy my mum and Alli. The worst is how I'm always touching my hair and fixing it. I've had that habit ever since I was a youngster. I also bite my nails. I can't stop, but I'm at least working on not doing it in public.

I spend a lot of time on my iPhone, maybe too much time. But it's the way I connect with my fans. I keep them updated on Twitter and Instagram — my favourite. I love taking pictures and sharing them. I'm a very artistic person, and photography is another important art form to me.

I don't play too many video games, other than with my little brother. I always feel like I should be doing something more productive with my time. Honestly, if I have downtime, I'd rather be outside, surfing or skating or hanging with my mates.

I try to surf as much as I can here in California. Nothing takes my mind off everything else the way surfing does. And I love going to the movies. One of my favourites is The Dark Knight with Heath Ledger. He was an Australian, and I think his interpretation of the Joker is amazing, one of the best roles ever played in a movie. I've seen that film more than 20 times. Unfortunately, he passed away, but he remains one of my biggest artistic inspirations with the way he put his heart and soul into every role he played. I also love a good comedy film. Will Ferrell cracks me up, especially in *Anchorman*.

And like most teenage guys, I love to eat — shamelessly. I love pasta with marinara sauce. And I'm addicted to chocolate, especially Kit Kats. I hate cheese, except on pizza. And I hate eggs. I eat junk food, but not too often if I can help it. At home, my mum cooks very healthily and tries to buy organic foods. I'm used to that from swimming. I was always aware of what I was eating and how it would fuel me to compete. But on the road, it's tougher. Sometimes the only options are fast food. Not that I don't love a Big Mac (with no cheese, of course) as much as the next guy — but after a while I go off it.

And, of course, music plays a huge part in my life. I used to listen to and perform with my music really loud in my headphones and ear monitors, and because of that I have tinnitus (a mild, constant ringing in my ears). Luckily it hasn't affected my career – but still, not smart. Now I have to be careful and make sure my volume isn't too loud. I love listening to Jack Johnson. I always have him on in my room whenever I'm in there or going to sleep. I like to go to sleep with mellow acoustic music on – it's soothing. It's probably not helping the tinnitus, though!

But it doesn't matter. Hearing a beautiful song just transports me. And I will listen to my favourite songs at any cost. Music is very powerful, and I'm just beginning to realise what an important job it is to create it.

**Below: On the set of the 'Summertime of Our Lives' video shoot.**

# Finding

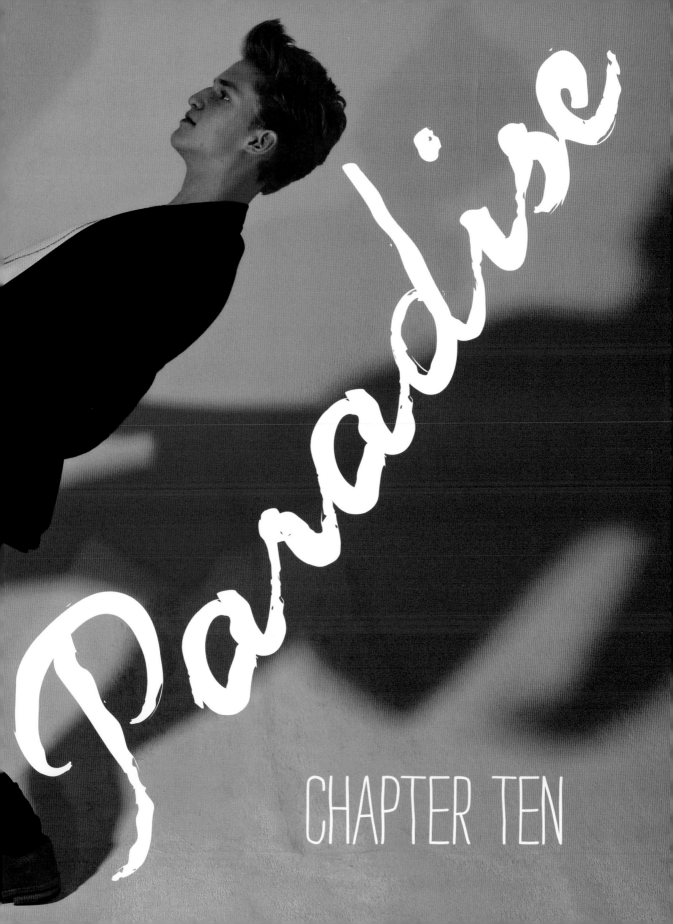

Paradise

CHAPTER TEN

# DEFINING MYSELF

When I first started out, I wasn't entirely sure of who I was musically, or as a person. I would question the way I dressed, even the way I spoke to people. A lot of that has to do with age. I think most teenagers probably question who they are. It's hard enough to figure out when you're leading a normal life. I had to figure it out in the spotlight. To be honest, until Matt and Scooter came into my career, the people around me were trying to tell me what to wear and how to be, and those two really helped me figure out who I was and backed my vision all the way. Above all, I knew that getting the chance to write and record my first proper studio album would be a great opportunity to define myself for the world – and for me.

So on *Paradise*, my first full-length album, I wanted to make the transition to more mature music – both with my lyrics and my sound. I now knew how I wanted to articulate my perspective. And I wanted to make sure that my new music would deliver for my fans.

The songs on *Paradise* showcase different styles of music that I've never really done before. There's a mix of laid-back beach tunes, like 'Got Me Good' and 'Summer Shade'. And then there's some real dance stuff and some creative, hybrid

MATT ALWAYS
SAYS, 'GREAT
ARTISTS CAN'T
BE PUT IN A BOX.'
THAT'S SOMETHING
I LIVE BY. I GUESS
I'LL JUST TAKE IT
AS IT COMES, AND
KEEP MATURING,
AND THAT WAY
MY MUSIC WILL
EVOLVE NATURALLY

tracks, like 'Wish U Were Here' and 'I Love Girls'. There's a part of me that wants to sit on the beach at a bonfire and listen to Jack Johnson, John Mayer, and Jason Mraz, and there's another part of me that wants to listen to MJ and Justin Timberlake, and get on the floor and dance. I love both. I want to do both. And for the first time, I think I can. Matt always says, 'Great artists can't be put in a box.' That's something I live by. I guess I'll just take it as it comes, and keep maturing, and that way my music will evolve naturally.

As you can probably tell, I really admire Justin Timberlake. And in particular, I respect how he transitioned from *The Mickey Mouse Club* to 'N Sync to creating his own unique sound as a solo artist. I saw how he developed and matured creatively. That rang true for me. There's always more to accomplish, more boundaries to push. And that's what I was feeling the whole time I was writing and recording *Paradise*.

Since *4U*, I've also learned a lot about the production side of recording. When I started out, the technical side of things seemed mysterious. Now I love to get behind the sound board at the studio and put my stamp on a song. I like being involved in every stage to make sure that the tracks are the best they can be. One thing I've discovered through the process is that I like telling stories and conveying emotion – that's why I love writing and singing the slower songs. This probably has a lot to do with my country music upbringing.

Choosing the songs for the album was a long process. I had a bunch of songs stacking up, maybe 30 or 40, that I considered for the EPs but didn't end up completing. Over time, we worked through a lot of them, and Matt and I decided on the ten best to start recording. Of course, we kept replacing the songs with new songs as we got closer to the release date. Never rest, I say. I think it's why the music just kept getting better. We decided on 15 that we were definitely happy with, and then ten finally made it onto the actual track listing.

Left: Visiting a radio station in Tokyo.
Right: Paradise tour.

I recorded the majority of the album in Hollywood, at the Atlantic Records studios. 'Wish U Were Here' was recorded with the producer Dr Luke at his house in Malibu. That time I stayed so late I fell asleep. Eventually he said, 'It's great. Go home and get some rest.' Dr Luke has worked with the majority of the biggest pop artists out there, so to hear that from him was pretty humbling. He's had more number-one hits on the radio over the past five years than any other producer.

If you really want to know the truth, I recorded 'Wish U Were Here' several times. The first time I recorded it with Luke's assistant engineer. After hearing the cut, Luke had some notes, so we went back to do it again. The second time I recorded it, I asked to give it a shot with my own engineer in Hollywood. I thought it came out great, but Luke still had comments about it (and I thought I was a perfectionist!). The third time, I went to a completely different studio, with another engineer. Luke was mostly satisfied with my third performance, yet still he wanted to make some improvements and alterations. So I went in for the fourth time to re-record – or at least perfect – it at his Malibu home studio, right on the beach. This time I was actually in the studio working with him in person. I literally sang it until I couldn't sing any more and I fell asleep. I like to think maybe it was the vibes of the ocean that crept into the booth and helped me finish the song. The ocean has always seemed to have that sort of quality for me.

As I write this book, I'm working on a new studio album, and I have been really picky in the studio, changing things, re-recording if I don't think it's good as it could be. I'd be so disappointed if I came to deliver the album and there were things that I thought I could have done better. I'm not going to get a second shot at this, and so I want to make sure everything is just the way I like it. When it comes to my music, I know exactly how I want it to sound. Sometimes it just takes work to get it to that point and to flesh out the vision. Even when everyone says it sounds great, let's move on, sometimes

Performing live is
my Paradise.

I still know I can do better. You just know when a song is done. It's when everything comes together, the beat is bumping right, and it all just feels smooth and perfect. I can't really describe how I know it's done. It just feels right.

An album is a real representation of who you are at that moment. I am sharing with my fans the experiences I've had and the type of person I am. And I think *Paradise* gives some real insights into that. 'Tears on Your Pillow' is one of my favourite songs off *Paradise*. My dad taught me how to treat women and how to be romantic. I think it's important to be a gentleman. I was raised that way. And the way my parents interact with each other inspires me. The song reflects that.

I also really love the song 'Gentleman'. I recorded this song in a unique way, and I think the effect is really different. First, I only used one single track of the guitar, and then I recorded one single take of the vocal. I didn't want to overproduce it. I didn't want too many harmonies or effects. The sound had to be clean and simple and intimate. I hoped it was a song my fans would like. And you did. So here's to you!

# NOTHING MAKES ME FEEL CONNECTED TO MY FANS OR TO THE MUSIC LIKE PERFORMING LIVE

I understand. It's just disappointing how much some people judge you on the basis of rumours.

Nothing makes me feel connected to my fans or to the music like performing live. It's an incredible feeling for me to walk out onstage and see thousands of fans waiting for me to perform. And I had the opportunity to share these new songs with fans live on my Welcome to Paradise tour. We travelled around the States in February 2012. I headlined and played to my biggest audiences yet. The first half of the tour sold out in two days, and we had to add a second round of shows in bigger venues to meet the demand.

It was crazy that all those people had bought tickets to see me! I know how I feel when I go and see a performance

by an artist I love. It's a powerful feeling. And for me to be able to give that feeling to thousands of people every night was an honour. It was incredible to see the reaction, the insane screaming and crying! All the girls were wearing Cody Simpson T-shirts. I loved that.

To have graduated from opening for someone else to performing for a crowd that had come to see me gave me an unbelievable feeling.

I wanted to give everyone in the audience a night to remember. A great concert isn't something you forget. I remember just about every concert that I've been to. It's a special night for the fans, and I want to win them over again. I want to leave my mark on every single person in the venue. That's all I think about when I walk out onstage.

I'm a big fan of Drake. I have all of his music. I saw him live at the Gibson Amphitheatre at Universal CityWalk in December 2011. Scooter got us tickets and Matt took me and Alli. I remember the feelings of excitement and anticipation as we got to our seats, right near the front. Being in the audience gave me a real insight into how my fans must feel at my shows.

Left: Chilling with my mate Josh.
Below: 'Come down off that roof, Cody!' Messing around at a video shoot.

ONCE I'M OUT
THERE, UNDER
THE LIGHTS
AND DOING
MY THING, I'M
COMPLETELY
CONFIDENT

It's a big part of the reason why I do everything I can to perform my best, night in, night out, at every show I do.

I know it's weird, but when I'm onstage, even though I sometimes can't see the audience past the first few rows because of the lights, I feel my fans. I'm connected to them. My focus narrows when I'm out there to just what's in front of me: the stage, the microphone, my guitar, the choreography. I'm entirely single-minded when I'm onstage. And even if I'm shy, reserved, or nervous right before I walk out of the wings, once I'm out there, under the lights and doing my thing, I'm completely confident. I work hard to make sure that what my fans are seeing is what I intended. And when the fans react to my dance moves or songs, it's awesome. It fuels me! It makes me want to never stop improving, to never stop performing.

Like most musicians, I have certain rituals or habits around a show that have sort of developed over time. Before a show, I like to be alone, if possible, to have time to think and psych myself up. Ninety-nine per cent of my performance is mental. No matter what's going on in my life – if I'm sick, or down, or whatever – I still have to go onstage and give it my best. So it takes me a minute to get that energy ready. I am never going to disappoint my fans.

My mind is usually racing before I go onstage. I check my hair and make sure my shoes are tied. Then I'll go over the set list quickly and look for any last-minute changes. Just before I walk onstage, I do a handshake with my security guard Jeff. We do the shake every night as the music is starting.

As I get to the stage, I feel the heat of the lights and the screams of the crowd. Then, as soon as I set foot into the spotlight, it all goes away – all the racing thoughts and worries – and I focus. It was the same thing when I was swimming at a competition. I would get up onto the blocks, and I'd adjust my suit and put my goggles on. But as soon as I touched the water, it all stopped. And it was just instinct. The bigger the competition, the faster I can swim – and the more guts I have to work for the win. It's the same with performing. I perform better in front of 20,000 people than I would in front of 200 people. The higher the stakes, the more I rise to the challenge.

On a photo shoot in NYC.

During my concerts, I'm completely in the moment. I try to feel every lyric and guitar riff. I don't even know what I'm thinking, other than trying to make it the best show possible. Sometimes, when there's a particularly high-energy, high-intensity dance break, I'll feel a certain thrill when I nail it and I can't help but smile.

I start to calm down pretty quickly when I come offstage after the show. As soon as I walk off, my security guard Jeff hands me a towel and a bottle of water, and he'll help stow my guitar away. Then he walks me to the dressing room. He's a funny guy and keeps everything light-hearted. I'll head to the dressing room, and put on some music while I shower and change.

How I feel after depends on how I think I did. As you'll have gathered, I'm a perfectionist. If I make a mistake, or more than one mistake, or if something goes wrong, I'll be quiet for a while. I'll know that I could have performed better, or that the show could have been better. I'm critical of myself. Even when others congratulate me or say it was an awesome show, it doesn't matter. I'll know when I've left something on the stage unfinished.

CHAPTER ELEVEN

On the
Road

# MY CREW

Not long after I came back from the Welcome to Paradise tour, I went back out on the road as a special guest on the Big Time Summer tour with the band Big Time Rush. We started in July 2012 and went all over the US and Canada, playing about 60 dates in three months at venues holding anything from 5,000 to 18,000 people. It was incredible! It was my first really big tour, and crowds of that size just got me so amped.

Nanna and Poppa came with us for a month of the tour with Big Time Rush. It was pretty awesome to show them how far I'd come. It must have been so hard for them when we moved, so I was stoked that they were proud of everything I'd achieved.

Sometimes it's just the fellas out on the road, but that time my whole family came. It was on that tour that our crew really grew, and with that growth I think some magic started to happen. Matt made some critical new additions – young guys that I could have fun with, and who wanted to be a part of something great and something special. Some of the notable new additions to that tour included guitarist Andrew Watt, who has become an important musical collaborator for me as well as a great mate.

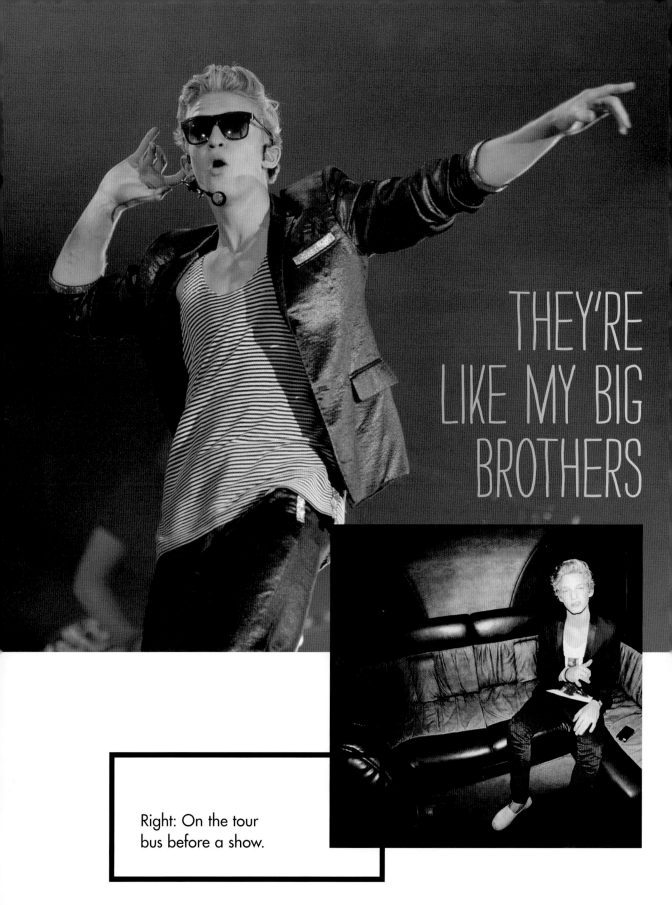

THEY'RE LIKE MY BIG BROTHERS

Right: On the tour bus before a show.

We also added Justin Stirling, a young guy who Matt found in Toronto. Justin is only three years older than me, so we could have been in high school together and, although he is really smart and hardworking, we sometimes act like we are. Justin is an aspiring artist manager. Matt took him under his wing and told me that he saw a lot of himself in Justin. He does a lot of different stuff on the road; some people in the touring business might refer to him as a road manager, but I just call him a great mate.

Matt also helped steal our videographer, Florent Déchard, who I call Flo, from Warner France. Flo is a gifted young director and photographer who agreed to come on and start shooting our web series for The Warner Sound as well as collecting photographs for this book. We also added my tour manager, Steven Welc, who takes care of so much for all of us. We would be lost without his organisation. The addition of that bunch to my current band and dancers created a new, special mix that made what could have been a long and gruelling tour an amazing summer to remember.

They're such a crazy bunch of guys to spend time with! I'm close to everyone, but I think I'm probably closest to Andrew, Flo, Justin, and Jeff, since they are all really near to me in age. Justin is from Canada and Flo is from France, so our crew is quite international, which I like since I, too, am not from the US. It's just great to be surrounded by some good, solid guys that I can trust and confide in. They're like my big brothers.

I really love being on the bus and on the road, partly because I have such a great band. Andrew, or Watt, as we call him — because his real last name is Wotman and he plays his music really loud — is the guy I write most of my songs with, usually while we're on the bus on tour, but some-times in the hotels. It often begins with us in the back of the tour bus. Watt will start things off with a cool guitar riff, and I'll sing some melodies over the top of it, and then we'll work

out the music and lyrics. Sometimes I'll have a concept percolating in my mind that I'll want to put to guitar; sometimes I will have the guitar and he will help with the melody.

The thing a lot of people hate about touring is sleeping in the coffin-like bunks of a moving bus. But I really like sleeping on the bus! I actually enjoy it more than sleeping at home or in the hotel. I like the little bunk, and the rocking of the bus sends me to sleep, as if I was on a boat. It's a good atmosphere with my band and the whole team. We have a lot of fun. We stay up late and wake up late. We'll turn in at 2 a.m. and wake up at midday sometimes, since we can't do much until the venue opens − and then I'll have to shower and get ready for the show. Oh, and school, of course! On off-days we often have to get up early and visit radio stations or local TV stations, which is not my favourite part of the job, but I guess I'm doing something right if they all want to talk to me.

On tour, I get to do meet-and-greets with fans before the show. I really enjoy being able to meet my biggest fans, to be able to really talk to them. My fans are the people who make what I do so worthwhile. And they sometimes bring really sweet gifts, like scrapbooks, T-shirts, and cool hats − plus lots of ketchup, obviously, since I eat it on everything. Once, I got these custom-painted Vans sneakers with beach scenes that reminded me of the scenery back home. So sick!

Sometimes fans will admit some really emotional and intense things − even that I've saved their lives. I don't always know what to do or what to say. It's hard for me to imagine that I can affect people in that way, but if I'm just being me and if I can help people, then it's awesome. It's easy to forget how much the songs mean to people.

Filming our Harlem Shake video on our European tour bus after leaving my show in Dublin.

# NEW HEIGHTS

My first album was a big moment and a big opportunity to share part of myself with the world. I had high hopes for *Paradise*, and I put immense pressure on myself to do my best. The success of the album meant more to me than I ever imagined. I really felt I'd discovered my sound and put together the right blend of songs to represent who I am. The album hit number one on the iTunes pop chart in the US and number one in Canada the day it came out, and number 27 on the Billboard Top 200 chart. Even more importantly, the response from my fans was overwhelming!

As hard as I work to connect to my fans and make sure I'm living up to their expectations, there are always critics. I accept that. It's a part of the job. I deal with it by ignoring it, mostly. I don't read negative criticism. I try to stay away from it online.

I'm hopeful that I will prove wrong some of the negative judgements I've received from the press. I want people to see me for the artist that I am and that I'm going to be. I want people to judge me for who I am, not on the basis of what they may read. I admit that before I was in the industry myself, I would read bad press about an artist and believe it all. I thought that if I read it in print, it must be true. But now

# WORKING WITH JUSTIN BIEBER

Touring with Justin Bieber was a dope experience. He's obviously one of the biggest artists in the world. The tour was a huge success in the US. Some of the dates sold out in less than an hour. From the moment when we arrived at the venue in Phoenix for the first show of the Believe tour you could tell that we were joining something epic, something that people were going to talk about for years to come. That night I felt like a part of history, opening up one of the biggest pop tours ever. It also motivated me even more to take my career even further.

Justin is very outgoing. I really enjoy his company and he's a lot of fun to kick back with. We're both busy, so we don't see each other too often, but he always makes an effort to check up on me. He's also three years older, but I think the age difference will narrow as we age. We get along very well, and spend some time together on tour, playing each other new music and asking one another's opinions.

I admire his performances and his success. Justin is super talented. And his vocal ability is outstanding. He has a great presence onstage, and I've definitely learned from watching him.

We're often compared, or mentioned in the same sentences, because we're coming through at the same time and we both emerged from YouTube. I respect him immensely for what he's doing, but we have different styles and different influences. I find a lot of my inspirations come from more contemporary artists like John Mayer, Jason Mraz, and Jack Johnson. From what Justin has mentioned, he is more influenced by R&B and hip-hop than I have been.

While on the tour, we hit the Barclays Center in Brooklyn, which had just opened to the public two months before the Believe tour show. That was an incredible night. I went on just before Justin, and our mate Jaden Smith opened the show. I remember, as I finished my performance, I was running offstage, when there, in the hallway, was the legend himself – Jay-Z. He had sold out eight dates there when the venue opened and he was backstage watching the show with Scooter, Will Smith, and a couple of other people. I did a double take as it was such a shock to see him at our show. He's one of those people you never expect to see just standing in a hallway talking. Scooter knew I wanted to say hello and invited me over.

I can't even remember what I said. I tried to keep it cool, but I was a little flustered, I think, and I was sweaty, having just come offstage. All I remember is that Mr Jay-Z said it was a great show. Now that's pretty incredible.

A few weeks after the Brooklyn show, we were in Miami, and Justin was filming a concert DVD. They were planning to film my set as well and include some of it on the DVD. There were a lot of cameras around and big rigs set up around the stage. I thought I should turn it up a bit and be on point. I was pretty hot for that one and thought it went really well. It was one of those nights when I walked offstage knowing I'd nailed it.

There are other nights, of course, when it just doesn't go as well. I struggle, and feel like I'm going through the motions, and I make a few mistakes. But then I try to think of it as the night I learn something. It's all part of my journey to be the best artist I can be.

Left: JB surprising me onstage at my LA show on the Paradise tour. Right: On a photo shoot in London.

I've heard it said that the real test of an artist is how you perform when everything goes wrong, rather than when everything's right. Well, I remember getting tested one night. I wear this strap around my torso that holds my ear-buds and headset pack. On this night, the pack fell out. I had the ear-buds in, but the cords were dangling, and I lost the pack on the ground and couldn't find it. I just kept going, singing and dancing, but I was trying to look around to find it. When I did, I broke from the dance routine and did a slide to the side of the stage to grab it. I managed to plug it back in and keep going. When I got offstage, I told my dancers about it, and they hadn't even noticed it had happened. It felt really good to know that I was able to handle something going wrong like that.

IT WAS AWESOME TO BE ON TOUR WITH JUSTIN BIEBER AND TO BE ABLE TO PROVE MYSELF AGAIN AND AGAIN, NIGHT AFTER NIGHT

# VISITING EUROPE

After covering the States, we headed to Europe for the second leg of the tour. I couldn't have been more stoked! It was my first time in Europe, and we were going to so many amazing cities – Dublin, Birmingham, Manchester, Glasgow, London, Antwerp, Utrecht, Munich, Cologne, Barcelona, and Paris. I was so excited to introduce myself to my fans over there and hopefully bring some new people to my music. Of course, it was a big tour and a big production, so it required a lot of preparation.

When I'm the opening act, I need to warm up the crowd, and that's my main objective. I play all of my biggest songs, to keep the energy really high.

It was awesome to be on tour with Justin Bieber and to be able to prove myself again and again, night after night. I know that not everyone who comes is a fan, but I want to make sure that everyone who leaves is one. I love to see the crowd go from subdued to on their feet. I love to see the energy rise when I turn the sceptics and haters into Angels and Gentlemen.

I was surprised by the reception I received in Europe, though. Judging by the volume of the screams, at least, I think audiences enjoyed the show. My Irish and UK fans have been particularly enthusiastic! They're so loud and welcoming wherever I go. Actually, sometimes they can be a bit too welcoming – we almost had to cancel one show mid-performance for fear of it becoming dangerous for the fans. The tour's only drawback for me was that I hate airports, and I don't like flying. I'm not scared; I've just done it so much that I'm sick of it. I much prefer being on the tour bus, with my band.

We didn't have time to do too much sightseeing, but we got to visit the *Harry Potter* set and saw Buckingham Palace and the Houses of Parliament. We took in the sights of Dublin before I was stopped by a mob of hundreds of fans on the street while shopping. I also got to see a lot of the beautiful architecture and old sights in Paris, Munich, and Barcelona. The architecture in Europe is breathtaking and inspiring.

It's amazing to have the chance to be a part of such a big tour. It's not just great exposure; it's about getting the chance to work with the best in the business – and to meet and make new fans. Also, visiting different countries, experiencing new cultures, and seeing new things helps to broaden my horizons, which in turn feeds into my music. It's a perfect circle.

Opening night in Glasgow, Scotland.

# To the Future

## CHAPTER TWELVE

# SURF-ISTICATED

When I'm not on tour or writing and recording music, I'm a pretty normal guy. I'm so not perfect, and I'm so not living the rock-star life every single day. Mum says I get a bit too highly strung about things. It's hard for me to take a complete break from music. I can't really relax. Even when I know I can really use some time away from it, most days I end up picking up the guitar or my ukulele and singing.

I'm like that with everything — even with an Instagram photo it will take me a while to think about the caption and the filter, to make sure I like it enough to post. Same with picking out clothes, especially for a big event. I get a lot of advice from Alli on what to wear — I usually end up going in and out of her room showing her different shirts until she yells at me to stop.

It's the same with music. Alli is always really honest with me. I'll play her early cuts of my songs, and she'll give me real feedback. We have a similar sense of style and taste in music, and I really rely on her — for more than just fashion advice. She's really the best. She's just very warm and kind. Sometimes I'd even say she's too nice. She's like my dad in that way. They're both so outgoing. I'm more like my mum. We're both much more sceptical and reserved.

# STYLE IS VERY IMPORTANT

I love that Alli is doing her own thing with videos and Twitter. I'm proud of her. She really has a lot going on for herself right now. She's the spokeswoman and model for Impress Broadway Nails and Pastry Shoes, two really fun brands that totally fit her personality. Alli and I have worked with Pastry almost as long as we have been in the US. They have supported lots of tours and always come up with brilliant ways for us to connect with our fans. They even helped her create her website, which has been a huge success. Last year she also acted in her first movie, *12 Dogs of Christmas: Great Puppy Rescue*. I loved hearing about her shoot days and experiences on set. I think it's awesome that we can share some of these one-of-a-kind experiences with one another.

And who knows what Tom will get himself into when he gets a bit older? The sky is the limit for him. Tom is an old soul and very intelligent. He's been travelling since he was so young and he's seen so much. Some of the things he says are just so profound that you question his age. How can something so remarkable come out of a nine-year-old boy? There are seven years between us, so we don't share friends or anything, the way Alli and I do. But I love spending time with him. He helps me relax and shut out business for a while. He's always waiting for me to get home from the studio so we can play *Call of Duty* for a bit.

I know that he looks up to me, so I try hard to be a good role model for him. I think it's important to pave a path that I would want him to walk down one day. I've noticed that girls often seem to be impressed by my relationship with Tom and my family. The few girls I've hung out with and brought around my family seem to like the way I treat my siblings. I just feel very lucky to have the family I do.

I wouldn't say that I'm high maintenance or focused on my looks. But, hey, style is very important. And I'm very picky about it. Like my hair, for example. It's definitely changed as I've got older and found my own unique look. I used to have more of the shaggy surfer 'do when I was younger and first moved from Australia. But now I like my hair a bit more slick and styled, and a little higher – inspired by Elvis Presley or James Dean. To get it that way, I go through a few jars of hair wax and grooming clay a month. When I'm on the road, I always bring at least two containers with me, but sometimes I still run out!

I like to describe my personal style as sophisticated surfer. I even came up with a term for it: 'surf-isticated' – I try to stay true to my beachy roots! Being in LA, I'm of course influenced by Hollywood, so I like to suit up. I try to create a mix. A surfer yet classy kind of look. I like it to be effortless, like James Dean. He completely embodied laid-back cool, which I totally admire.

Of course, my man Justin Timberlake also has a pretty sophisticated style. I like what he wears onstage – usually a suit, although lately he has traded it in for the tuxedo. He must have been influenced by my *Paradise* album cover!

Speaking of suits and fashion, Marc Jacobs is my favourite designer. My stylist, David Royer, works with him and his company to supply most of my red-carpet looks and stage wear. When I went to the Grammys earlier this year, I wore Marc Jacobs – trousers, a beach-inspired tan button-up shirt, and a very cool grey jacket. For a big night like that, you have to make sure you look fly and fresh.

I usually wear a casual suit that looks a little funky – you know, something shiny and maybe a bold colour for the stage, with a tank underneath. The stuff I wear onstage is a more extravagant version of my real-life style. We found this rare Marc Jacobs suit – all shiny blue. We put a nautical striped tank underneath and added gold shoes. It was pretty sweet!

I TRY TO
STAY TRUE
TO MY
BEACHY
ROOTS

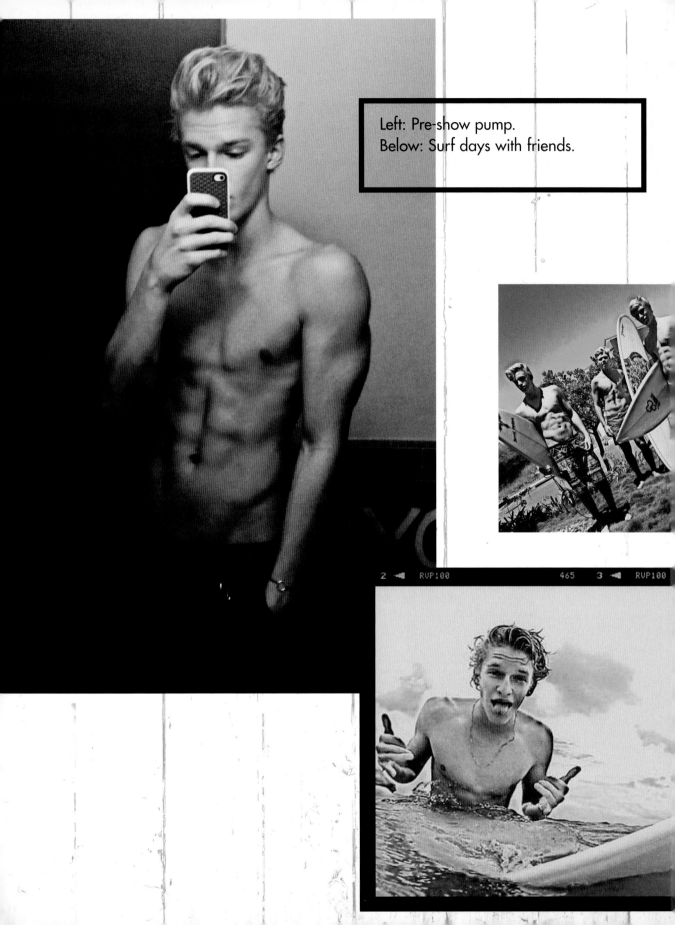

Left: Pre-show pump.
Below: Surf days with friends.

In real life, I wear boat shoes and a lot of surf brands, like Billabong and Vans. I get a lot of clothes, like T-shirts and casual stuff, from stores that my mates own on the Gold Coast. It's always good to support the local surf shops.

None of that would look good if I didn't keep up my appearance physically. My security guard, Jeff, is also a personal trainer, so he tries to keep me healthy on the road. He helps me with workouts. I work out whenever I can, and it's actually easier when I'm travelling with him than when I'm at home. I feel like I'm busier when I'm at home than I am when I'm on tour. At home I'm doing more with school, the studio, and rehearsals and everything. On the road, it's all about the show and the fans.

I travel with these adjustable weights that we'll break out if we can't get to the hotel gym. And sometimes we'll do a makeshift workout on the bus, with dips in between the bunks and push-ups and stuff. I've always been very active. I like it that way.

I haven't done a swimming training session since I was back home. It's probably been about three years. Sometimes I do a couple of laps in a hotel pool, but obviously nothing at all like I did back home. I realise how far off I am now compared to when I was training at my peak. I miss the competitions and stuff. The training was pretty intense, but I do miss it. When I was watching Michael Phelps and Ryan Lochte swim in the Olympics last year, I could feel that familiar sense of competition and adrenalin, as if I was competing, too. When I get back in the pool I sometimes race my dad and stuff, and the feeling does come back, for sure. There's nothing in the world quite like the thrill of a race. I miss it. I suspect I always will.

# PARADISE 2

As I write, I'm back in the studio recording my latest album, *Paradise: Part 2*. I hope it demonstrates my continuing evolution as an artist. Music is a powerful tool of expression, and I think this album is my most personal and revealing album to date. It's a little more mature, naturally, because I'm growing up and I want my music to reflect that. *Paradise* had a pretty even mix of acoustic, groovy songs and more up-tempo dance songs. *Paradise: Part 2* will incorporate more of that groovy guitar vibe. I'm writing constantly, and as I keep evolving, the songs I'm coming up with are tending to be more in that acoustic guitar style. It's shaping up into what I want it to be. It really reflects my vision for what a great album should be.

For a pop artist like myself, it's important to continually shape and reshape my sound. I know that might worry my fans who like me just the way I am, but I think they'll really enjoy the direction in which I'm heading. I'm hoping they'll want to come along for the ride.

My dream? To collaborate with either Jack Johnson or Justin Timberlake one day. Justin Timberlake is just such a good entertainer. He's a total inspiration, especially his live performances. I'd also love to write songs with Jack Johnson. Maybe on the beach in Hawaii, where he lives. I love his way with lyrics. Pop star or not, he's a total poet. Such a genius.

As I wrote songs for the album, I focused on more mature subject matter. And as a result, I think, the sound itself has become more polished, more sophisticated. For example, 'Stolen' is a moody, emotional song inspired by my experience when I fell for a girl who had a boyfriend. Also, the song 'Neck Kisses' is a lot sexier than anything I've sung before. I think both show my growth, and I hope that my fans will enjoy listening to them as much as I enjoyed writing and singing them.

Acoustic set with
Andrew Watt.

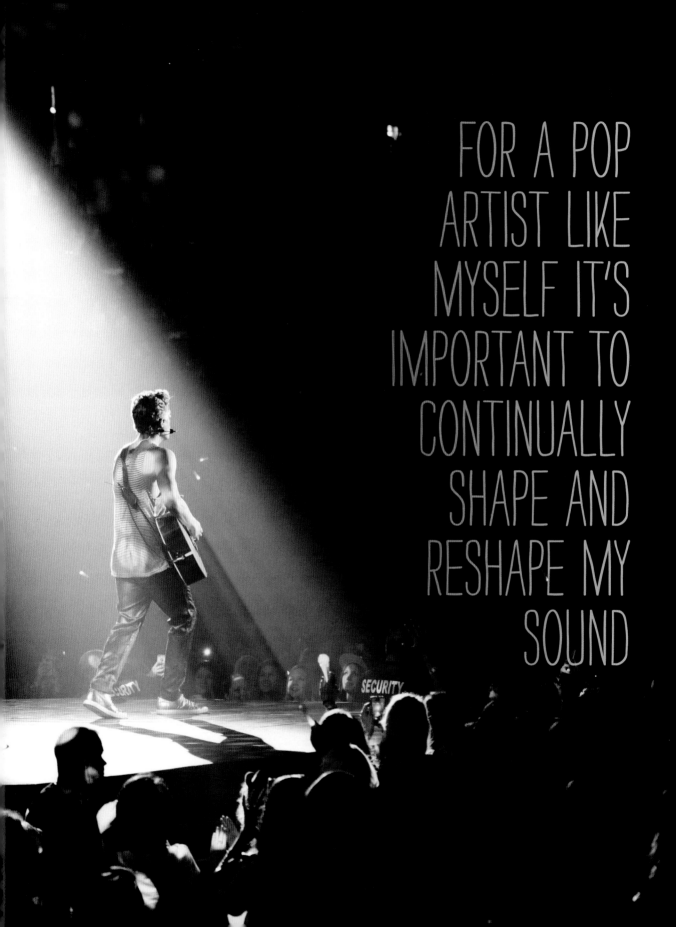

FOR A POP ARTIST LIKE MYSELF IT'S IMPORTANT TO CONTINUALLY SHAPE AND RESHAPE MY SOUND

lusion

I COULD HAVE HAD A BRIGHT FUTURE IN SWIMMING, BUT I KNOW I MADE THE RIGHT DECISION

# THE FUTURE

Sometimes I think about where I would be now if all of this had never happened. Where would I be if I hadn't moved to LA and pursued music? Obviously I think about what could have happened with my swimming. Perhaps I focus too much on this question. I'm passionate about music and creating something important. But I was also right on the cusp of achieving some of my major dreams in swimming.

I know that if I had stayed swimming in Australia and never taken the chance in signing with a record label, I would be asking myself the same kind of question: what would have happened with music? But I think the feelings of regret – and wondering if I'd made the right choice – would be much more intense if it was the other way around.

If you asked me whether I would rather be headlining a sold-out arena tour around the world or winning a gold medal at the Olympics, my answer would be headlining the arena tour around the world. Winning a race is conquering something. Playing a great show is giving something to the fans. It's a form of expression. I could have had a bright future in swimming, but I know I made the right decision.

When I was offered a record deal in the States and the chance to create songs that express who I am and what I'm about, I knew it meant giving up swimming. I had been training hard and felt so close to achieving my goals. Saying goodbye was a pretty radical move. To swim in the Olympics for Australia was my dream, and one that was in my sights. But an opportunity to sign with a major record label – well, that's the kind of chance that only comes along once in a lifetime. So I took it.

The water and the music are both a big part of who I am and where I came from. It was a difficult decision to leave one of them behind. But it was the best decision I ever made.

I feel blessed in so many ways, but especially for the unconditional support of my family as I follow my dreams. My parents, brother, and sister uprooted their lives and moved to Los Angeles for an adventure. And that's certainly what we've had so far! From red carpets and touring throughout Europe to being followed by fans in a supermarket – they've stood by me through it all.

And still, I know I'm at the very beginning. It was a lot of hustling during those first two years to kick it off and prove myself. Now that I've established myself I feel a lot more freedom musically than I did when I first started out. Now I can be true to myself, write my own songs, and really express myself. It takes a while to be trusted creatively.

And there's so much more I still have to show the world. Having had the experiences I've had and having the fans I have, I wouldn't trade it for anything in the world. It's paradise. It really is. And I'm only just getting started. Trust me.

# THANK YOU

First and foremost, I want to extend the deepest thank-you to my fans. You are the ones reading this book right now and if it wasn't for you, none of this would be possible. From the very bottom of my heart, thank you for supporting me at every turn. You give me the confidence, strength, and motivation to continue to work hard and be the best person and artist I can possibly be. It's a special feeling, which I can hardly describe, knowing that I have you with me always. You come to the shows, you listen to the music, you have my back, and so much more. This book is for you. It's for you to get to know me better, it's for you to understand where I came from and where I want to go. Please continue to join me on this journey.

Thank you to my managers Matt Graham and Scooter Braun and the rest of the amazing team at Scooter Braun Management, including but not limited to Allison Kaye, Brad Haugen, and Scott Manson, for believing in me and guiding me at every turn. Also, thank you to the team at Primary Wave Management. Thank you to David Loeffler and Randy Phillips and the rest of the AEG family for giving me the tools to become the best entertainer I can be. My incredible choreographer Ed Moore. Cameron Duddy and Harper Smith for being rad. Jeff Traynor for teaching me to be a beast. My band, dancers, and crew for touring with me. Tina Fasbender, Lauren Adovasio, and Jon Nussbaum at Fasbender & Associates for looking after me. Thank you to my legal team, Aaron Rosenberg, Josh Karp, and Eric Greenspan, for always protecting me.

I'd also like to thank my tour crew, including my videographer and photographer Florent Déchard who captured many of the incredible images in this book, my tour manager Steven Welc, road manager Justin Stirling, and guitarist/

musical director Andrew Watt! You fellas make touring such an awesome experience. So many hilarious memories!

A special thank-you to my incredible label, Atlantic Records/Warner Music Group, and to everyone who helps out in New York/Los Angeles and offices all across the world. Julie Greenwald, Craig Kallman, Chris Stang, Pete Ganbarg, Chris Morris, Aaron Bay-Schuck, Mike Caren, Jon Lewis, Andrea Ganis, Michele Cranford, Torsten Luth, Christine Goyette, Christina Kotsamanidis, Chelsey Northern, Sheila Richman, David Saslow, Jason Pleskow, Danielle Geiger, Dane Venable, Harlan Frey, Sara Nemerov, Jack McMorrow, Adam Abramson, Matt Engelman, Nick Bilardello, Andrew Schenkel, Camille Hackney, Jonathan Feldman, Brad Rains, Phil Botti, Erica Bellarosa, Maria Gagliese, and so many others.

Lastly, I'd like to share my thanks and appreciation with my family. Mum, Dad, sister Alli, and brother Tom, I wouldn't be in this position if it wasn't for your support and encouragement. You've given up an astounding amount in order for me to pursue my musical and artistic endeavours, and for that I will be forever grateful. You're by my side every step of the way, and I thank you for keeping my feet on the ground and my head out of the clouds! Matt Graham, my manager and the big brother I never had, what would I do without you?! Thank you for believing in me and working so hard. We're in this together! I also appreciate the oceans of priceless advice you've drowned me in, applicable to many important aspects of my life: music, work, and the ladies.

**Cheers,**

**P.S. Do Something Cool**

HarperCollins*Publishers*
77–85 Fulham Palace Road,
Hammersmith, London W6 8JB

www.harpercollins.co.uk

10 9 8 7 6 5 4 3 2 1

Design: Ben Gardiner and Lucy Sykes-Thompson

All photographs supplied courtesy of Cody Simpson and his management team unless otherwise stated.

Images on pp. 11, 12 (top),18–19, 25 (bottom), 31 (bottom), 38–39, 44–45, 47 (bottom right), 50–51, 55 (right), 74–75, 85 (top left), 90–91, 98, 115, 119, 120 (top left), 129 (middle left), 132, 133, 134 (right), 136, 137, 138, 139, 140–141, 142 (top), 149, 152, 153, 158, 159, 165, 172 (bottom left), 176–177, 179, 183, 184–185, 186, 190–191, 192, 195,196 (left), 200–201, 202 (top), 205, 210–211, 213, 221, 222–223, 227, 228–229, 234–235, 238–239 © Florent Déchard

Images on pp. 2, 4, 6, 8–9, 12 (bottom right), 14, 16–17, 42–43, 48, 62–63, 64, 73, 76–77, 78, 93, 100–101, 106, 116–117, 127–128, 146–147, 156–157, 160–161, 162, 174, 178, 180–181, 198–199, 209 (right), 214–215, 218, 230–231 and 236 © Ellis Parrinder

Images on pp. 1 and 3 © www.shutterstock.com

A catalogue record of this book is available from the British Library

ISBN 978-0-00-752056-5

Printed and bound in China by RR Donnelley

**MIX**
Paper from
responsible sources
www.fsc.org  **FSC™ C007454**

FSC™ is a non-profit international organisation established to promote the responsible management of the world's forests. Products carrying the FSC label are independently certified to assure consumers that they come from forests that are managed to meet the social, economic and ecological needs of present and future generations, and other controlled sources.

Find out more about HarperCollins and the environment at
**www.harpercollins.co.uk/green**